COOKING
WITH
CHIMINEAS

COOKING WITH CHIMINEAS

150 delicious recipes for barbecuing, grilling, roasting and smoking

Wendy Sweetser

NEW HOLLAND

First published in 2007 by New Holland Publishers (UK) Ltd
London • Cape Town • Sydney • Auckland

Garfield House
86-88 Edgware Road
London W2 2EA
www.newhollandpublishers.com

80 McKenzie Street
Cape Town 8001
South Africa

Level 1, Unit 4
14 Aquatic Drive
Frenchs Forest, NSW 2086
Australia

218 Lake Road
Northcote
Auckland
New Zealand

1 3 5 7 9 10 8 6 4 2

ISBN 978 1 84537 724 3

Senior Editors: Caroline Blake, Naomi Waters
Design: Casebourne Rose Design Associates
Photography: Ian Garlick
Editorial Direction: Rosemary Wilkinson
Production: Hazel Kirkman

Reproduction by Modern Age Repro, Hong Kong
Printed and bound by Star Standard Industries, Singapore

ACKNOWLEDGEMENT
The author and publishers would like to express their gratitude to Jay Emery of Dingley Dell
Enterprises for supplying the Bushman Burner (see front cover) that was used to test the
recipes in this book.

contents

INTRODUCTION

We all agree that good food tastes even better when eaten outside but, with unpredictable weather, barbecuing can often be a chilly and sometimes solitary business as the cook shivers in the garden, turning over the burgers and sausages, while everyone else knocks back a few drinks in the comfort and warmth of the kitchen indoors.

Recently a new type of outdoor burner called a chiminea has begun to appear in our garden centres and hardware stores. As the burner can be fuelled by wood and charcoal briquettes it makes a very effective patio heater and dining outside becomes a realistic year-round option.

However, a chiminea is a lot more than just a patio heater because it is designed to be used as a cooker as well, and it is a lot more versatile than a traditional barbecue. In addition to a rack in the oven for chargrilling and roasting, a pot can be placed on a trivet on top of the chimney so you can steam, simmer, smoke and stir-fry as well.

This book tells you all you need to know about chimineas – what they are, where they came from, the different types available and how to look after them – but principally it's about food and the fun you can have cooking on them.

From formal dining to party food, snacks and deliciously indulgent desserts, there's something for everyone, even vegetarians who can so often feel left out at a barbecue party. Inevitably, once you've started experimenting with your chiminea you'll be hooked and – who knows? – you might even discover it's the only cooker you'll ever need.

What is a chiminea?

Chimineas originate in Mexico, where tribesmen first developed them as heaters and ovens for baking bread. Consisting of a chimney or "stack" above a round, open-fronted "oven", the first ones were hand-built using wet clay, but they were fragile and liable to crack if drenched with a sudden downpour of rain when alight. Mexican rainfall is quite low and the warm climate meant that a radiant glow was sufficient to keep a family warm. With a ready supply of mud and river clay to build another chiminea whenever it was needed, more durable building materials were not a priority. Some modern chimineas are still made of terracotta but other, longer-lasting materials, such as cast iron and industrial clay are also now used.

The Bushman Burner

All the recipes in this book were tested on a Quickfire Classic Bushman Burner (see the photograph on the cover). This burner has a much larger mouth than other models so is best suited to

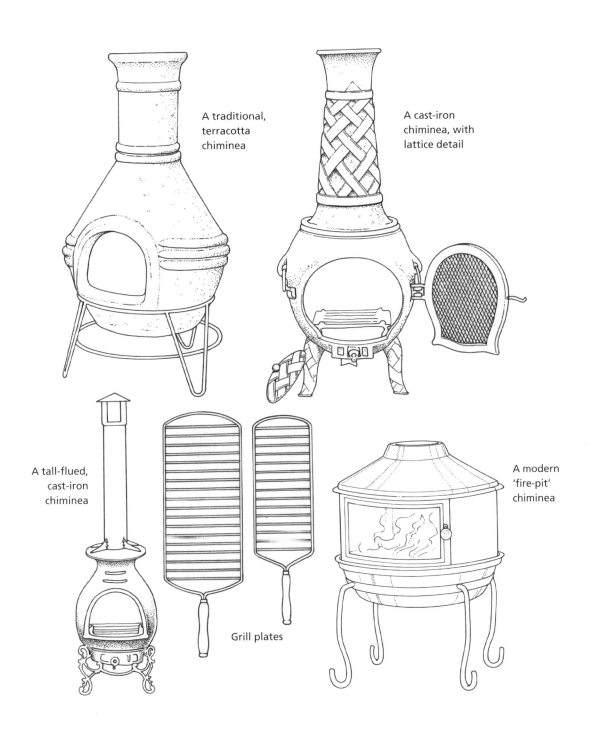

A traditional, terracotta chiminea

A cast-iron chiminea, with lattice detail

A tall-flued, cast-iron chiminea

Grill plates

A modern 'fire-pit' chiminea

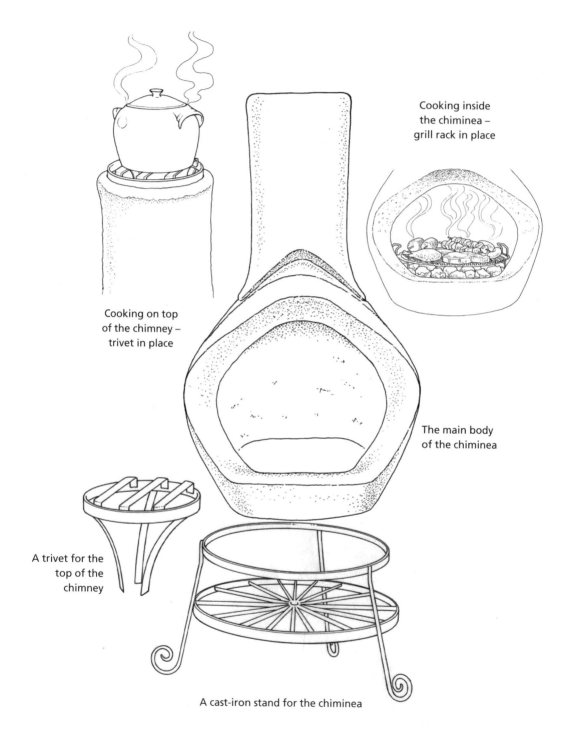

Cooking inside
the chiminea –
grill rack in place

Cooking on top
of the chimney –
trivet in place

The main body
of the chiminea

A trivet for the
top of the
chimney

A cast-iron stand for the chiminea

barbecuing as the coals and flame patterns are clearly visible. For cooking the fire grate needs to be taken out and replaced with a cooking grid, which can be lifted in and out easily.

Can I cook on any type of chiminea?
Yes. Bushman Burners however, are specifically designed for cooking as they have a much larger 'mouth'. They are also very effective patio heaters.

Can I use it all the year round?
Unless they are sealed on the outside with a special sealant, terracotta chimineas are really designed for summer use only as leaving them out during the winter can cause them to crack or break. Cast-iron chimineas are likely to rust if left outside in damp conditions for long periods and not protected by special paint or a cover. Bushman Burners are made from a special blend of industrial clays reinforced with wire mesh that holds them together and enables them to withstand the vagaries of the British winter. The burners can safely be left outside all year round, although it's advisable to keep the chimney covered to stop rainwater building up inside and to use a cover when the burner is not in use for long periods to discourage birds or small animals from taking up residence inside. Another advantage of a Bushman Burner is that you will not burn yourself if you touch the outside of it, unlike a chiminea made of terracotta or cast iron.

How do I cook on my chiminea?
If it has a fire grate lift this out and stack charcoal in the bottom of the stove as you would for an ordinary barbecue, with a few twists of paper or dry kindling between. Light the charcoal and leave it until the flames burn out and the charcoal is covered with white ash and glows red – about 30 minutes. Insert a barbecue grill rack the same size as your chiminea oven, and you are ready to cook.

How do I control the cooking temperature?
The heat can't be turned up or down as on a conventional oven, but its intensity can be adjusted. If you find the grill rack is too close to the coals it can be raised up on a trivet or bricks. When grilling small items, such as burgers, steaks or kebabs, position the charcoal directly under the grill so the food cooks quickly. For an indirect heat that is less intense, stack the charcoal on either side of the bottom of the stove, leaving a gap in the middle.

What fuel does a chiminea burn?
For cooking, only charcoal or logs can be burnt. If using only as a heater, smokeless coal can be burnt in a Bushman Burner, but not in a cast-iron or terracotta chiminea as they could break.

Where is the best place to position my chiminea?
Chimineas are best sited on the edge of a patio away from trees or

overhanging branches. As cast-iron chimineas get extremely hot when lit, they should be placed well away from any inflammable material or plants.

Apart from grilling food on the rack, how else can I cook on it?

One useful accessory is a trivet to fit into the top of the chimney for use as a pot stand for stir-frying, steaming, smoking and slow-cooking dishes like casseroles. Joints of meat or whole chickens can be roasted on a rotisserie placed in front of the oven. When cooking on top of the stove or spit roasting in front of the oven, logs must be used for fuel as the heat produced by glowing charcoal will not be fierce enough. Unlike with charcoal, you can start to cook as soon as the logs are alight.

What pots do I use for cooking on top of the chiminea?

Any flameproof pot is suitable as long as it is not your newest and best as the fire will make it black and sooty. Cast-iron pots are best as they are an excellent conductor of heat, don't lose moisture and can be heated to high temperatures.

If the rack fills the oven space, how do I add extra fuel during cooking?

Buy a hinged grill that allows the sides of the rack to be lifted and extra charcoal dropped in. With logs,

it shouldn't be necessary to add more as they will burn for longer and give out a greater heat.

What cooking utensils do I need?

Similar utensils to those you would use for a barbecue. Long-handled tongs, a poker to move coals and logs, oven gloves to protect your hands, a water spray to douse any flare-ups, a wire brush to scrub the bars of the rack, and a fire extinguisher – just in case.

A griddle or cast-iron frying pan, a wok, casserole and a saucepan with a tight-fitting lid for the top will enable you to cook most dishes.

Metal skewers are more practical for kebabs as wooden ones tend to burn even when pre-soaked in cold water. If using wooden skewers, wrap small pieces of foil round their ends to protect them.

A folding, hinged rack is useful for cooking fish or other small, delicate items as the food can be turned in one go without the risk of it breaking up.

How long should I marinate food?

Poultry and meat benefit from long marinating before cooking to absorb as much flavour as possible so allow several hours or overnight if possible. Fish and shellfish shouldn't be marinated for longer than 1 hour or the flesh will start to lose flavour and texture. When marinating food, cover the bowl or dish with clingfilm and keep in a cool place, preferably the refrigerator, but remove it 30 minutes before cooking, so that the food can come back to room temperature.

How accurate can cooking times be when using a chiminea?

The cooking times given for the recipes in this book should only be used as a guide as it's difficult to give precise timings when cooking over an open fire. A lot depends on the heat of the fire, the thickness of the food being cooked, how close it is to the heat source and how well done people like their meat or fish. When grilling chicken, it's advisable to use thighs, breasts, drumsticks or wings as they cook more quickly and evenly. When cooking chicken legs, it's a good idea to partially cook them in a conventional oven and simply finish them off on the chiminea rack. When making a casserole on top of the stove, calculate the cooking time from when the food comes to a simmer.

Where can I get one?

The Quickfire Bushman Burner costs £335 and there are others available in Mini (£275), Midi (£300) and Maxi (£350) sizes – prices include stand, lid and fire grate. The burners can be bought direct from Dingley Dell Enterprises, PO Box 3534, Kidderminster DY14 9ZE (01905 621636) or from retail outlets around the UK. For more information about Bushman Burners and local stockists, visit www.bushmanburners.co.uk. Terracotta and cast-iron chimineas can be bought from garden centres and DIY stores, and on the internet.

A few notes on the recipes:

• Jars of ready-made garlic, ginger, lemon grass and chilli purées are convenient to use and blend easily into sauces and marinades and are suggested for many of the recipes. However, use the fresh ingredients if you prefer.

• Where a particular oil, such as extra virgin olive oil or sunflower oil, is important for the flavour of a finished dish, this is specified. Otherwise use whatever oil you have available.

• Salt is listed in some recipes where it enhances the flavour of a dish but, with many of us keeping an eye on our salt intake, and marinade ingredients like soy sauce already being salty, please feel free to season dishes according to personal taste.

1 starters and light meals

Tangy turkey kebabs
Chilli scallops with lime and coriander
Lime and ginger-glazed fish skewers
Wasabi beef bites in lettuce cups
Seared prawn, papaya and cucumber salad
Asparagus and Serrano ham wraps
Parma ham, fig and Roquefort nests
Oriental chicken salad
Lemon grass prawn sticks
Roasted vegetable bruschetta
Ginger and green tea-smoked salmon
Grilled sardines with herbs and shallot vinaigrette
Thai-style mussels
Crab cakes with mint and coriander
King prawns with salsa verde
Golden tikka bites
Hoi sin ribs

Mozzarella and pesto bread
Sausage and apple burgers
Sweet and sour chicken kebabs
Indian spiced chicken burgers
New York bagels
Maple-glazed drumsticks
Best-ever BLTs
Cumberland sausage with sage and apple
Corn on the cob with mint and chilli butter
Lamb, mint and feta burgers
Cheese and chorizo quesadillas
Turkey and cheese burgers
Ciabatta stuffed with Parma ham and mozzarella
Grilled aubergine and salami focaccia
Plum lamb kebabs
Quarter pounders
Hot-dog baguettes
Chicken fajitas

Tangy turkey kebabs

In the last few years turkey has transformed its image from a Christmas-only bird to a versatile meat that can be enjoyed all year round. Many different cuts of turkey are available and breast steaks cook quickly, have very little fat and are much cheaper than their chicken equivalents.

PREPARATION TIME: 10 MINUTES + MARINATING

COOKING TIME: 5 MINUTES

SERVES 4

2 Tbsp dark soy sauce
1 tsp creamed horseradish
2 Tbsp soft brown sugar
2 Tbsp lemon juice
700g (1lb 9oz) turkey breast steaks, cut into bite-sized chunks
1 green pepper, deseeded and cut into chunks

TO SERVE
Romesco sauce (see page 154)
Mixed salad

1 In a bowl, whisk together the soy sauce, horseradish, brown sugar and lemon juice, stirring until the sugar dissolves. Add the turkey chunks, turning them over so they are well coated. Leave to marinate for 3–4 hours.

2 Lift the turkey from the marinade and thread on to skewers with the chunks of pepper.

3 Cook on the grill rack for about 5 minutes until the turkey is cooked through, turning over once or twice and brushing with any marinade left in the dish.

 tip

Instead of turkey, you could make these kebabs with pork, chicken or lamb.

Chilli scallops with lime and coriander

It's important not to overcook scallops as their delicate flesh will quickly dry out and become tough.
Heat the griddle until it is very hot so the scallops start to sizzle as soon as you place them on it.

PREPARATION TIME: 10 MINUTES + MARINATING

COOKING TIME: LESS THAN 5 MINUTES

SERVES 4

12 large scallops, corals on or removed as preferred
1 large red chilli, deseeded and very finely chopped
Finely grated rind and juice of 1 lime
1 Tbsp chopped fresh coriander
Freshly ground black pepper

TO SERVE
Wild rocket leaves, cherry tomatoes and spring onions

1 Put the scallops in a shallow dish. Whisk together the chopped chilli, lime rind and juice, coriander and pepper and pour the mixture over the scallops, turning them over so they are evenly coated.

2 Leave to marinate for 30 minutes.

3 Lift the scallops from the marinade and sear on a very hot griddle for 1 minute on each side until they are lightly browned and just cooked.

4 Pour over the marinade left in the dish and serve immediately on a bed of wild rocket leaves, tossed with halved cherry tomatoes and shredded spring onions. Spoon the juices over the scallops

 tip

If you're worried that the scallops will stick to the griddle, lightly brush it with oil first.

Lime and ginger-glazed fish skewers

Use a meaty, firm-fleshed fish for this recipe, such as monkfish or swordfish, as softer fish such as haddock or cod will flake and fall off the skewers as it cooks. Golden turmeric adds a splash of colour as well as a touch of spice.

PREPARATION TIME: 15 MINUTES + MARINATING

COOKING TIME: LESS THAN 10 MINUTES

SERVES 4

450g (1lb) firm fish fillets, skinned
Juice of 2 limes
1 tsp fresh ginger purée
$1/2$ tsp ground turmeric
5 Tbsp orange juice
1 tsp brown sugar
12 cherry tomatoes
4 lime leaves or small bay leaves

TO SERVE
Salad of mixed leaves

1 Cut the fish into 2.5cm (1in) chunks and spread them out in a shallow dish.

2 Mix together the lime juice, ginger, turmeric, orange juice and sugar, stirring until the sugar dissolves. Pour the mixture over the fish, turning the pieces so they are well coated. Leave to marinate for 30 minutes.

3 Thread the fish pieces on to skewers with the cherry tomatoes and lime leaves or bay leaves. Grill on the rack for about 5–6 minutes or until the pieces of fish turn opaque, turning the skewers over once or twice, and basting with any marinade left in the dish. Serve hot with a salad of mixed leaves.

tip

The cherry tomatoes need to be ripe but firm so they don't collapse during cooking. You could substitute cubes of red pepper, button mushrooms or chunks of courgette for the tomatoes.

Wasabi beef bites in lettuce cups

Although similar to British horseradish, green Japanese wasabi is more fragrant and less harsh in flavour, although still hot and peppery. It can be bought as a paste or powder; the paste is usually sold in a toothpaste-like plastic tube.

PREPARATION TIME: 15 MINUTES + STANDING

COOKING TIME: LESS THAN 10 MINUTES

SERVES 4

1 thick sirloin steak
Freshly ground black pepper
1 Tbsp chilli oil
4 Tbsp light olive oil
1 Tbsp white wine vinegar
$^1/_2$ tsp wasabi paste
$^1/_4$ tsp caster sugar
4 cherry tomatoes, quartered
$^1/_4$ green pepper, deseeded and finely chopped
1 shallot, peeled and finely chopped
12 little gem lettuce leaves

1 Season the steak with pepper, brush it on both sides with the chilli oil and cook on the grill rack for 2 minutes on each side or until cooked to your liking. Remove the steak from the rack and leave to rest for 10 minutes. Trim off any fat and cut the steak into really thin slices across the grain of the meat.

2 Whisk together the olive oil, vinegar, wasabi paste and sugar until smooth and the sugar has dissolved.

3 Arrange the lettuce leaves on serving plates and fill with the cherry tomatoes, green pepper, shallot and steak. Spoon over the dressing and serve at once.

tip

Instead of sirloin, you could use rump or fillet steak. Look for steak that's a deep, red-brown rather than bright red as it will have been hung for longer and be succulent and tender.

Seared prawn, papaya and cucumber salad

This winning combination of succulent prawns, sweet papaya and crunchy cucumber makes an attractive and refreshing starter. Papaya is available most of the year, imported into the UK from tropical climes.

PREPARATION TIME: 10 MINUTES + MARINATING

COOKING TIME: 1–2 MINUTES

SERVES 4

400g (14oz) raw tiger prawns, peeled
2 Tbsp lime juice
1 tsp wholegrain mustard
1 tsp clear honey
1 Tbsp chopped fresh mint
4 Tbsp light olive oil
Freshly ground black pepper
1 ripe papaya, peeled, deseeded and cut into bite-sized pieces
1/4 cucumber, sliced

TO SERVE
Crusty bread

1 Put the prawns in a shallow dish. Whisk together the lime juice, mustard, honey, mint, 3 Tbsp olive oil and pepper, and pour over the prawns, turning them over until they are coated. Marinate for 30 minutes.

2 Arrange the papaya and cucumber on serving plates. Lift the prawns from the marinade. Heat the remaining 1 Tbsp of olive oil in a griddle or hot plate on the grill rack and, when really hot, add the prawns. Cook for 1–2 minutes until they turn pink and opaque.

3 Pour the marinade left in the dish over the prawns, allow it to bubble for a few seconds and then spoon the prawns and the pan juices over the papaya and cucumber. Serve at once with crusty bread.

tip

Oval in shape with a yellowy-green skin, the soft dark orange flesh of the papaya becomes sweet, juicy and aromatic when ripe. To prepare, slice the fruit in half lengthways and scoop out the small, shiny black seeds in the middle with a spoon.

Asparagus and Serrano ham wraps

Spanish Serrano ham is produced from the prized White-Foot Pigs that roam the cork oak forests of the south and west of the country getting fat on a diet of acorns. The ham is first cured and then air-dried, a process that can take anything from a few months to three years.

PREPARATION TIME: 10 MINUTES

COOKING TIME: 5 MINUTES

MAKES 12

12 long asparagus spears, woody ends trimmed off
2 Tbsp extra virgin olive oil
12 wafer-thin slices Serrano ham
12 large basil leaves
Freshly ground black pepper

TO SERVE
Tomato chilli mayonnaise (see page 150)

1 Brush the asparagus spears with the olive oil.

2 Lay a slice of ham on a board, place a basil leaf and asparagus spear on top and wrap the ham round the spear. Repeat with the remaining ingredients.

3 Season the wraps with freshly ground black pepper and grill on the rack for about 5 minutes, turning once or twice until the ham is crisp.

4 Serve with tomato chilli mayonnaise.

 tip

An easy starter or pre-dinner nibble to serve with drinks. Look for long, fairly thin asparagus spears as very thick ones will take too long to tenderize on the grill and the ham, meanwhile, could burn.

Parma ham, fig and Roquefort nests

The sweet flesh of ripe figs makes the perfect foil for the salty, blue cheese. This makes an excellent late-summer starter when the luscious black figs from Turkey arrive in our shops.

PREPARATION TIME: 15 MINUTES

COOKING TIME: 3–4 MINUTES

SERVES 4

8 large ripe but firm figs
115g (4oz) Roquefort cheese
4 walnut halves, chopped
1 tsp snipped fresh chives
8 wafer-thin slices Parma ham

1 Cut a cross in the top of each fig and open out as much as you can by holding the bottom of the fig gently, and pressing with your thumb and index fingers.

2 In a small bowl, mash the cheese and mix in the walnuts and chives. Spoon a little of the mixture into the centre of each fig.

3 Wrap a slice of ham around each fig, folding it over if necessary so the fig protrudes through the top of the ham.

4 Warm through on the grill rack or on a hot plate on top for 3–4 minutes, just long enough for the ham to start to crisp and the figs to heat up so they melt the cheese a little. Serve at once.

 ## tip

If you're worried these nests might break up or fall apart if placed directly on the rack, cook them on a cast-iron hot plate. The nests only need a few minutes to sizzle the ham and heat the other ingredients through, so make sure that they don't overcook.

Oriental chicken salad

Slicing the green beans in half lengthways is done for aesthetic effect in this recipe as it makes them look more interesting, rather than culinary necessity. If you're short of time or just can't be bothered, leave the beans whole – the salad will taste equally good!

PREPARATION TIME: 15 MINUTES + MARINATING

COOKING TIME: 15 MINUTES

SERVES 4

2 boneless chicken breasts, skinned
3 Tbsp light soy sauce
1 tsp toasted sesame oil
1 tsp soft brown sugar
2 Tbsp rice vinegar or white wine vinegar
2 Tbsp oil
1 celery stick, sliced
1 yellow pepper, deseeded and sliced
50g (2oz) green beans, halved lengthways and blanched for 30 seconds
$1/4$ cucumber, cut into matchsticks
2 radishes, sliced

1 Place the chicken breasts in a shallow dish. Mix together the soy sauce, sesame oil, sugar, vinegar and oil, stirring until the sugar dissolves. Spoon half over the chicken, turning the breasts over until coated. Leave the chicken to marinate for 1 hour. Set the rest of the marinade mixture to one side.

2 Grill the chicken on the rack for about 15 minutes until cooked through, basting with any marinade left in the dish and turning over once or twice.

3 Toss the celery, yellow pepper, green beans, cucumber and radishes with the remaining half of the marinade mixture. Cut the chicken into slices, arrange on top of the salad and serve.

 ## tip

The crunchy salad ingredients contrast well with the sweet, juicy chicken, which should be sliced thinly and served while still warm. Blanch the beans in advance and cool under cold water so they retain their bright green colour and stay crisp.

Lemon grass prawn sticks

Lemon grass adds a delicate Far Eastern aroma to dishes and goes particularly well with seafood as its flavour isn't overpowering. Instead of sweet chilli dipping sauce as an accompaniment, plum sauce or a bowl of dark soy sauce could be served.

PREPARATION TIME: 10 MINUTES + MARINATING

COOKING TIME: 5 MINUTES

SERVES 4

12 large raw prawns, peeled and deveined
1 tsp sugar
2 Tbsp rice vinegar
2 Tbsp Thai fish sauce (nam pla)
1 garlic clove, peeled and crushed
1 tsp fresh lemon grass purée

TO SERVE
Sweet chilli dipping sauce (see page 151)

1 Put the prawns in a bowl. Stir the sugar into the rice vinegar until it dissolves, then stir in the fish sauce, garlic and lemon grass and pour over the prawns, turning over until they are coated. Leave to marinate for 1 hour.

2 Thread the prawns on to short skewers and grill on the rack for about 5 minutes until they turn pink, brushing with any marinade left in the dish.

3 Serve hot with Sweet chilli dipping sauce.

 tip

Short lengths of fresh lemon grass stalk could be used as skewers. If you split the stalks lengthways to make them easier to thread through the prawns, they'll become floppy and difficult to turn over, so would be best cooked on a griddle rather than directly on the rack.

Roasted vegetable bruschetta

This recipe can be served as a starter or turned into a light lunch dish with the addition of crumbled feta, Gorgonzola or goat's cheese and thin slices of Parma or Serrano ham.

PREPARATION TIME: 10 MINUTES

COOKING TIME: 10 MINUTES

SERVES 4

$1/2$ aubergine, thinly sliced
1 courgette, thinly sliced
1 orange pepper, deseeded and cut into 8 slices
2 garlic cloves, peeled and chopped
Juice of 1 lemon
4 Tbsp extra virgin olive oil
Freshly ground black pepper
8 baby plum tomatoes, halved
4 slices country bread, toasted
2 Tbsp sun-dried tomato purée

TO SERVE
Houmous
Aubergine, garlic and coriander mash (see page 135)

1 Put the aubergine slices, courgette slices, pepper slices, garlic, lemon juice and olive oil in a bowl and season with plenty of freshly ground black pepper. Toss the vegetables until they are coated in the oil.

2 Heat a cast iron griddle or hot plate on the grill rack, add the vegetables and roast for 5 minutes, turning the slices over once or twice. Tuck the tomato halves in amongst the vegetables and roast for a further 5 minutes until everything is tender and lightly scorched at the edges.

3 Spread the toasted bread with the sun-dried tomato purée. Cut each slice in half, place on serving plates and spoon over the vegetables, drizzling over any juices left in the pan.

tip

These small vegetable pieces must be roasted on a griddle or hot plate because they'll shrink and fall through into the coals if placed directly on the grill rack.

Ginger and green tea-smoked salmon

In Asia, tea-smoking was originally a good way to preserve fish or chicken but these days it's used to add flavour and a deliciously smoky aroma to food. Commercial smokers can be used, but this recipe is an easy way to smoke the fish in a wok on top of the chiminea.

PREPARATION TIME: 15 MINUTES + MARINATING AND STANDING

COOKING TIME: 5 MINUTES

SERVES 4

2 Tbsp oil
1 tsp fresh ginger purée
2 Tbsp rice vinegar
1 tsp light soy sauce
4 x 150g (5oz) salmon fillets

TEA-SMOKING MIX
3 Tbsp caster sugar
3 Tbsp plain flour
4 Tbsp green tea leaves
1 cinnamon stick, broken into 3 pieces

1 Mix together the oil, ginger purée, rice vinegar and soy sauce. Lay the salmon in a shallow dish and spoon over the ginger mixture, turning the fillets over so they are coated. Set aside to marinate for 1 hour.

2 Line a wok with a sheet of foil large enough for the ends to hang over the sides. Mix the tea-smoking ingredients together and spoon into the bottom of the wok.

3 Stand a metal rack in the wok so it sits about 5cm (2in) above the smoking mix. Lift the salmon from the marinade, pat dry with kitchen paper and place on the rack, skin side down.

4 Cover the wok with a lid and fold over the edges of the foil to make a tight seal. Stand the wok on top of the chiminea and once you can smell smoke, leave it to cook for 5 minutes.

5 Remove from the chiminea and allow to stand for 5 minutes before taking off the lid. Serve the salmon hot or cold.

Grilled sardines with herbs and shallot vinaigrette

Although sold descaled, most sardines still have a few scales stuck to their skin when you buy them, so remove these by holding each fish by the tail over a sheet of newspaper and gently rubbing the scales off with your fingers.

PREPARATION TIME: 10 MINUTES

COOKING TIME: 5 MINUTES

SERVES 4

8 fresh sardines, whole or filleted
8 tbsp olive oil
Fresh herb sprigs, e.g. rosemary, fennel, thyme
2 Tbsp coarse sea salt
2 Tbsp red wine vinegar
1 shallot, peeled and very finely chopped
Freshly ground black pepper

1 Brush the sardines with 2 Tbsp olive oil and place on the grill rack. Tuck herb sprigs between them and sprinkle with the sea salt.

2 Grill for about 5 minutes until cooked, turning over half way.

3 Whisk the remaining olive oil with the vinegar and chopped shallot and season with freshly ground black pepper.

4 Transfer the cooked sardines to serving plates, spoon over the vinaigrette and serve at once.

 ## tip

You can either cook the sardines whole, in which case score the flesh several times on each side with a sharp knife, or fillet them. To fillet, remove the heads from the sardines and cut along the underside. Open the fish out and place on a board skin side up. Press down the backbone of each with your fingers to loosen it, then turn over and snip the backbone just above the tail with kitchen scissors. Carefully pull out the backbone and ribs in one go.

Thai-style mussels

Mussels are usually sold ready to cook but if you buy ones that haven't been cleaned, pull away the thread-like "beards" and rinse them well in cold water to remove any sand trapped inside.

PREPARATION TIME: 10 MINUTES

COOKING TIME: LESS THAN 10 MINUTES

SERVES 4

4 spring onions, chopped
1 lemon grass stalk, split in half lengthways
4 lime leaves or finely grated rind of 1 lime
Juice of 2 limes
4 Tbsp chopped fresh coriander
1 red chilli, deseeded and very finely chopped
150ml (5fl oz) fish stock
2kg (4lb 8oz) mussels, in their shells
150ml (5fl oz) coconut milk

1 Put the spring onions, lemon grass, lime leaves or rind, lime juice, 2 Tbsp coriander, the chopped chilli and fish stock in a large pan or wok with a lid and place on top of the chiminea.

2 Bring the mixture to the boil, add the mussels and cover the pan. Cook for about 5 minutes, shaking the pan regularly, until the mussel shells have opened. Discard any mussels that remain tightly shut once cooked, as they won't be safe to eat.

3 Lift out the mussels with a slotted spoon and pile into serving bowls. Fish out and discard the lemon grass, put the pan back on the chiminea and let the liquid bubble for 2 minutes. Whisk in the coconut milk and bring the liquid back to a simmer. Don't let it boil too hard as this will cause the milk to break down and lose its creamy consistency. Pour over the mussels.

4 Sprinkle with the remaining coriander and serve at once.

Crab cakes with mint and coriander

It's best to cook these cakes on a griddle. If placed directly on the rack, they are fiddly to turn over.

PREPARATION TIME: 15 MINUTES + CHILLING

COOKING TIME: LESS THAN 10 MINUTES

SERVES 6

450g (1lb) white crabmeat
2 Tbsp dry breadcrumbs
4 spring onions, trimmed and very finely chopped
2 tsp Dijon mustard
1 Tbsp lemon juice
2 Tbsp chopped fresh coriander
1 Tbsp chopped fresh mint
1 egg, beaten
Freshly ground black pepper
4 Tbsp plain flour
2 Tbsp oil
50g (2oz) butter

TO SERVE
Salad garnish
Garlic and lemon mayonnaise (see page 150)

1 Flake the crabmeat into a bowl, checking for any small pieces of shell and removing them.

2 Add the breadcrumbs, spring onions, mustard, lemon juice and herbs and stir until evenly mixed.

3 Stir in the beaten egg to bind the mixture together and season with the black pepper.

4 Shape the mixture into 12 flat cakes and dust them with flour on both sides. Put in a single layer on a plate, cover with clingfilm and chill for 2 hours or until ready to cook.

5 Heat the oil and butter in a small pan until the butter melts and brush over the crab cakes. Cook the cakes for 2–3 minutes on each side on a hot plate or griddle on the rack until golden brown. Serve with a small salad garnish and garlic and lemon mayonnaise.

King prawns with salsa verde

The mix of herbs suggested for the salsa verde in this recipe can be varied according to what you have available, but use herbs with soft leaves such as tarragon, marjoram, chives or chervil, rather than tougher-leafed varieties like rosemary or thyme.

PREPARATION TIME: 10 MINUTES

COOKING TIME: LESS THAN 5 MINUTES

SERVES 4

2 tsp Dijon mustard
4 Tbsp extra virgin olive oil
2 Tbsp chopped fresh coriander
1 Tbsp chopped fresh basil
2 Tbsp chopped fresh parsley
1 fat garlic clove, peeled and finely chopped
12 raw king prawns, unpeeled
Freshly ground black pepper
1 lemon, cut into wedges

1 To make the salsa verde, whisk the mustard and olive oil together until smooth, then whisk in the coriander, basil, parsley and garlic. Set aside.

2 Grill the prawns on the rack for 1–2 minutes on each side or until they turn pink and opaque.

3 Remove the prawns from the rack and, as soon as they are cool enough to handle, peel off the shells and remove the heads and tails.

4 Season the prawns with plenty of freshly ground black pepper, squeeze over the lemon wedges and serve with the salsa verde.

 tip

Leaving the shells on the prawns helps protect their delicate flesh as, like all shellfish, if prawns overcook they become horribly tough and tasteless. The salsa verde can be made in advance; if it separates on standing, simply whisk it back together just before serving.

Golden tikka bites

You can use other curry pastes instead of tikka if you prefer. Vindaloo or Madras will suit those who like things hot, something more subtle such as korma or tandoori for those who don't.

PREPARATION TIME: 10 MINUTES + MARINATING

COOKING TIME: LESS THAN 10 MINUTES

SERVES 4

2 boneless chicken breasts, skinned and cut into 2.5cm (1in) cubes
100g (3^1/$_2$oz) thick natural yogurt
1 Tbsp tikka curry paste
1 Tbsp chopped fresh mint
2 tsp lemon juice
2 Tbsp oil
^{1}/$_4$ cucumber, cut into chunks
4 cherry tomatoes, halved

TO SERVE
Mango chutney

1 Thread the chicken on to eight small skewers, leaving space at the pointed end for a piece of cucumber and half a cherry tomato. Lay the skewers side by side in a shallow dish.

2 Mix together the yogurt, curry paste, mint, lemon juice and oil and spoon over the chicken, turning the skewers over so the meat is well coated. Leave to marinate for 3–4 hours or until ready to cook.

3 Grill the chicken on the rack for 5–6 minutes until cooked through, turning the skewers over once or twice during cooking.

4 Remove from the grill and add a chunk of cucumber and half a cherry tomato to each skewer. Serve warm with mango chutney.

Hoi sin ribs

Pork ribs are cut from the lower part of the belly and/or loin. They should be eaten with your fingers, so make sure there are plenty of paper napkins to hand.

PREPARATION TIME: 20 MINUTES + COOLING AND MARINATING

COOKING TIME: 1 HOUR 5 MINUTES

SERVES 4

900g (2lb) pork stick ribs
Approx. 600ml (1pt) chicken stock
2 Tbsp tomato ketchup
4 Tbsp hoi sin sauce
1 Tbsp dark soy sauce

1 Simmer the ribs in the stock for 1 hour, following the recipe instructions for sticky Chinese ribs (see page 52).

2 Once cool, transfer the ribs to a dish. Mix together the tomato ketchup, hoi sin sauce and soy sauce and spoon over the ribs, turning them over so they are well coated. Leave to marinate for 3–4 hours.

3 Grill the ribs on the rack for about 5 minutes until dark brown and glistening with the sauce, turning them over once and basting with any marinade left in the dish.

tip

Hoi sin, also known as Chinese barbecue sauce, is thick, dark, sweet sauce made with soya beans, spices and garlic. It can be brushed or basted over pork or chicken and cooks to a finger lickin' sticky glaze.

Mozzarella and pesto bread

Mozzarella for cooking is sold in blocks, and is dryer than the firmer, softer balls of cheese packed in water and used for salads. French bread or ciabatta are best for this recipe but any crusty loaf would be suitable, provided it will fit on the grill rack. The bread makes a good accompaniment to burgers and sausages if you're cooking a more substantial meal.

PREPARATION TIME: 10 MINUTES

COOKING TIME: 15 MINUTES

SERVES 6

1 French stick, large ciabatta or half baguette
2–3 Tbsp pesto
175g (6oz) cooking mozzarella cheese, thinly sliced
3 Tbsp extra virgin olive oil

1 Cut the loaf in half lengthways and spread the bottom half with pesto. Top with the cheese slices and cover with the other half of the loaf.

2 Wrap the bread in foil, sealing the parcel along the top so it is easy to open and place on the grill rack for 10 minutes. Remove and cut open the foil so the top of the loaf is exposed.

3 Drizzle over the olive oil and return to the rack for 5 minutes or until the top of the loaf is crisp.

4 Unwrap and cut into thick slices.

tip

Have a board and sharp serrated knife on a table near the chiminea so you can cut up the load and serve it whilst it's still warm. If you're having a party, make up several loaves with different flavourings, such as sun-dried tomato purée, tapenade or anchovy paste.

Sausage and apple burgers

These are filling fare for a brunch or late breakfast party, accompanied by spicy tomato sauce for grown ups and ketchup for the kids. Serve them in burger buns or with roasted sweet potato wedges.

PREPARATION TIME: 15 MINUTES

COOKING TIME: 15 MINUTES

MAKES 6

700g (1lb 9oz) sausagemeat
1 Tbsp chopped fresh sage or 1 tsp dried sage
1 small onion, peeled and finely chopped
1 dessert apple, peeled, cored and grated
1 Tbsp Dijon mustard
Freshly ground black pepper

TO SERVE
Spicy tomato sauce (see page 163)
Roasted sweet potato wedges (see page 139)

1 In a bowl, mix together the sausagemeat, sage, onion, apple and mustard. Season with freshly ground black pepper.

2 With damp hands, shape the mixture into six burger patties.

3 Cook on the grill rack for about 15 minutes, turning the burgers over once or twice until well browned and cooked through.

4 Serve with roasted sweet potato wedges and spicy tomato sauce.

 tip

Use a firm variety of apple for the burgers, such as
Cox or Granny Smith as an apple with soft flesh,
such as Bramley or Queen will become too soft and
disintegrate when cooked.

Sweet-and-sour chicken kebabs

These kebabs really benefit from being prepared well in advance so they have time to absorb all the flavours from the marinade. The recipe could also be made with pork, turkey breast or lean lamb.

PREPARATION TIME: 10 MINUTES + MARINATING

COOKING TIME: 5 MINUTES

SERVES 4

4 boneless chicken breasts, skinned and cut bite-sized pieces
2 Tbsp clear honey
2 Tbsp dark soy sauce
2 Tbsp dry sherry
2 Tbsp tomato ketchup

1 Put the chicken in a bowl or shallow dish. Mix together the honey, soy sauce, sherry and ketchup until evenly combined and pour over the chicken, turning the pieces over until they are coated. Leave to marinate for 6 hours, or overnight if possible.

2 Thread the chicken on to skewers and cook on the grill rack for about 5 minutes, turning them over once or twice and basting with any remaining marinade as they cook. Keep a close eye on the kebabs whilst they're grilling as the chicken needs to be cooked through but not overdone as it will quickly dry out and become tough.

3 Check the kebabs after 5 minutes by cutting into the thickest piece of meat on a skewer and return to the rack for another minute or so if it is not quite ready.

Indian-spiced chicken burgers

Balti curry paste is medium-hot in strength so substitute fiery vindaloo or mild korma if you prefer. The red pepper needs to be very finely chopped so the pieces don't fall out when the burgers are grilled.

PREPARATION TIME: 15 MINUTES + CHILLING

COOKING TIME: 10–15 MINUTES

SERVES 4

450g (1lb) chicken mince
4 spring onions, trimmed and finely chopped
$1/2$ red pepper, deseeded and finely chopped
2 Tbsp balti curry paste
1 Tbsp lemon juice
2 Tbsp oil

TO SERVE
4 burger buns or naan breads, toasted
Rocket leaves
Cucumber slices
Raita (natural yogurt mixed with chopped fresh mint)
Mango chutney

1 In a bowl, mix together the chicken, spring onions, red pepper, balti curry paste and lemon juice. Shape the mixture into four burgers, pressing the ingredients together firmly, and chill for 1 hour or until ready to cook.

2 Brush the burgers on both sides with the oil and cook on the grill rack for 10–15 minutes until brown and cooked through, turning over once.

3 Serve in burger buns or naan bread topped with rocket leaves and cucumber slices. Add raita and mango chutney as preferred.

 tip

Curry paste adds a touch of spice to the mild flavour of the chicken. The burgers can also be made using turkey mince.

New York bagels

American mustard is mild and sweet and comes in an easy-to-use squeezy bottle – ideal for al fresco eating. The blue cheese needs to be firm enough to crumble so choose Stilton or Roquefort in preference to a creamy Dolce Latte.

PREPARATION TIME: 15 MINUTES + PLUS STANDING

COOKING TIME: LESS THAN 15 MINUTES

SERVES 4

4 fillet steaks
2 tsp creamed horseradish
115g (4oz) cream cheese
115g (4oz) blue cheese, e.g. Stilton or Roquefort, crumbled
4 bagels, split
4 lettuce leaves
1 onion, peeled and thinly sliced into rings
8 baby gherkins or 2 dill pickles, sliced
American mustard

1 Cook the steaks on the grill rack for 5 minutes on each side or until done to your liking. Remove and place on a board or plate, cover with foil and leave somewhere warm for 10 minutes.

2 Mash together the horseradish, cream cheese and blue cheese. Lightly toast the bagels on the grill rack and slice the steaks as thinly as possible.

3 Spread the bottom halves of the bagels with the horseradish mixture and arrange the lettuce leaves and steak slices on top. Separate the onion slices into rings and add to the bagels with the gherkins or dill pickle slices. Add a squeeze of American mustard, replace the bagel lids and serve.

tip

The steak can be cooked directly on the grill rack or a cast iron griddle placed on the rack if you prefer. Leaving the meat to stand somewhere warm for 10 minutes will make it easy to slice thinly.

Maple-glazed drumsticks

These are certain to be a hit with children and adults alike and, as they're eaten with the fingers, no knives, forks or plates, means less washing up too!

PREPARATION TIME: 10 MINUTES + MARINATING

COOKING TIME: 25–30 MINUTES

SERVES 4

8 chicken drumsticks
4 Tbsp tomato ketchup
2 Tbsp maple syrup
1 Tbsp vinegar
2 Tbsp oil

1 Using a sharp knife, score the flesh of each drumstick several times across the grain of the meat. Arrange the drumsticks in a single layer in a shallow dish.

2 Mix together the ketchup, maple syrup, vinegar and oil and spoon over the chicken, turning the drumsticks over so they are well coated in the marinade. Set aside to marinate for 3–4 hours.

3 Grill the drumsticks on the rack for 25–30 minutes or until cooked through, turning over occasionally and basting with any marinade left in the dish.

tip

Scoring the flesh of the chicken helps it absorb more of the flavours of the marinade and also speeds up the cooking time. Leave the skin on the drumsticks or remove it as preferred.

Best-ever BLTs

If you're not a fan of the peanut butter included in this recipe, spread the bread with tomato chutney, sweet pickle or chunky cranberry sauce.

PREPARATION TIME: 10 MINUTES

COOKING TIME: 10 MINUTES

SERVES 2

2 tomatoes, sliced
1 large dill pickle, sliced
4 lettuce leaves
4 rashers back bacon, halved
6 slices bread, cut fairly thinly
2 Tbsp crunchy peanut butter

TO SERVE
Coleslaw (see page 140)

1 Slice the tomatoes and dill pickle, separate the lettuce leaves and put them to one side. This will enable the sandwiches to be assembled straight away while the cooked bacon and toast are still hot.

2 Grill the bacon rashers on a cast iron hot plate or griddle on the rack for about 10 minutes until brown and crisp, turning over once.

3 Toast the bread slices on the rack and spread four of the slices with the peanut butter.

4 Layer the bread with the lettuce, bacon rashers, tomato and dill pickle slices to make two sandwiches. Cut each into four and skewer the triangles with cocktail sticks. Serve with coleslaw.

tip

It is best to grill the bacon in a cast-iron pan because if it's placed directly on the rack any fat that drips down on to the coals will cause flames to leap up and scorch the thin rashers.

Cumberland sausage with sage and apple

Traditional Cumberland sausage comes curled in a spiral and a large one will feed two people. The heat under the grill rack must not be too fierce or the sausage will brown too much before it's cooked through.

PREPARATION TIME: 10 MINUTES

COOKING TIME: ABOUT 20 MINUTES

SERVES 4

1 large Cumberland sausage, secured with a skewer
1 Tbsp smooth mustard (English, if you like things hot!)
1 tsp vinegar or lemon juice
1 tsp dried sage
2 Granny Smith apples, or other apples with a tart taste
25g (1oz) butter, melted
2 tsp sugar

TO SERVE
Jacket potatoes (see page 141)

1 Cook the sausage on the grill rack for 10 minutes, turning it over halfway. The skewer is there so that the spiral doesn't uncurl as it cooks.

2 Mix together the mustard, vinegar or lemon juice and sage and brush half over the sausage. Grill for 5 minutes, turn it over and brush with the remaining sage mixture.

3 Grill for a further 5 minutes or until cooked through.

4 When the sausage is nearly ready, halve and core the apples, but don't peel them. Brush the apples with the melted butter and sprinkle with the sugar. Place on the grill around the sausage and cook for 2–3 minutes until lightly caramelized but not falling apart.

5 Serve the sausage with Jacket potatoes and the caramelized apples.

 ## tip

If fresh sage isn't available, substitute another herb such as thyme or mint.

Corn on the cob with mint and chilli butter

If the mint and chilli butter in this recipe is not to your taste, try one of the other flavours on page 149. The corn cobs are dipped in cold water to stop the husks scorching and to keep the cobs moist.

PREPARATION TIME: 10 MINUTES + CHILLING AND SOAKING

COOKING TIME: 25 MINUTES

SERVES 4

115g (4oz) butter, softened
2 Tbsp chopped fresh mint
1 small red chilli, deseeded and very finely chopped or 1 tsp fresh chilli
    purée
4 corn cobs in their husks

1 In a bowl, mash the butter with a fork until soft. Beat with a wooden spoon until creamy and then gradually beat in the mint and chilli until combined.

2 Spoon the butter on to a sheet of clingfilm and shape into a small log. Wrap the clingfilm tightly round the butter and chill in the refrigerator for 2 hours or until ready to serve.

3 Put the corn cobs in their husks in a large bowl of cold water and leave to soak for 30 minutes. Drain, carefully peel back the husks – but without removing them – and pull away the long, silky threads attached to the cobs.

4 Fold the husks back over the cobs and grill them on the rack for 15 minutes, turning once or twice. Take the cobs off the rack, dip them into cold water and grill for a further 10 minutes, turning once or twice.

5 Once the cobs are tender, peel away the husks and discard. Unwrap the butter, cut into four equal slices and serve over the hot cobs.

 ## tip

An alternative method to steps 3 and 4 (above) is to remove the husks and pre-cook the corn cobs in a pan of boiling water for 7–8 minutes until tender or use defrosted frozen cobs. Place the cobs on the rack, brush with the melted chilli butter and grill for about 10 minutes, turning occasionally.

Lamb, mint and feta burgers

These lamb burgers are given a delicious Greek twist with the addition of tangy feta cheese and fresh mint.

PREPARATION TIME: 10 MINUTES + CHILLING

COOKING TIME: 15 MINUTES

SERVES 4

115g (4oz) feta cheese
450g (1lb) lean lamb mince
1 Tbsp finely chopped fresh mint
Freshly ground black pepper

TO SERVE
1 small aubergine, cut into thin slices
2 Tbsp olive oil
4 burger buns, lightly toasted
1 small red onion, peeled and sliced into rings
Tomato pickle

1 Drain any water off the feta and blot with kitchen towel. Crumble the feta and put in a bowl. Mix in the lamb, mint, feta and seasoning until evenly combined. With damp hands, shape the mixture into four burger patties and chill for 1 hour or until ready to cook.

2 Grill the burgers on the rack for 5 minutes on each side until well browned. Remove and keep warm.

3 Brush the aubergine slices with the olive oil and cook on the rack for about 5 minutes until tender.

4 Layer the aubergine slices, burgers and onion rings on the bottom half of the buns, add a spoonful of tomato pickle and the bun lids and serve.

 tip

If you have problems making neat, even-sized burgers that don't fall apart on the grill, stand a large pastry cutter on a foil-lined baking sheet and spoon the mince into it, pressing the meat down so you get a good burger shape. Alternatively, it can be worth investing in a proper burger press. Always chill burgers for at least 1 hour before cooking so they have time to firm up.

Cheese and chorizo quesadillas

Quesadillas are a Mexican snack made by sandwiching soft flour tortillas with a variety of fillings such as cheese, spicy sausage, chillies, herbs and even mashed potato, and then frying the stack until crisp. This recipe uses chorizo to give the filling a hint of spice, but add a finely chopped green chilli if you want more heat.

PREPARATION TIME: 5 MINUTES

COOKING TIME: LESS THAN 5 MINUTES

MAKES 12 WEDGES

2 Tbsp olive oil
2 soft flour tortillas
175g (6oz) Cheddar cheese, grated or thinly sliced
115g (4oz) chorizo sausage, chopped or thinly sliced
2 Tbsp chopped fresh coriander

TO SERVE
Spicy tomato sauce (see page 163)
or Romesco sauce (see page 154)
Guacamole (see page 153)

1 Brush a cast-iron frying pan with olive oil and heat on top of the chiminea or the grill rack.

2 Place one tortilla in the pan and cover with the cheese and chorizo. Scatter over the coriander and lay the second tortilla on top to cover the filling.

3 Cook for 2 minutes or until the tortilla is crisp underneath. Carefully slide the stack out of the pan on to a plate, put another plate on top and turn it over. Slide the stack back into the pan and cook for a further 1–2 minutes to crisp the other tortilla.

4 Slide out of the pan back on to a plate and cut into 12 wedges with a sharp knife or kitchen scissors. Serve hot.

 tip

These wedges make an unusual pre-dinner appetizer served with dips and sauces.

Turkey and cheese burgers

Turkey mince is available from most butchers and supermarket meat counters or you can make your own using either breast or leg meat. If chopping the meat in a food processor, take care not to overdo it or you'll end up with a mush!

PREPARATION TIME: 15 MINUTES + CHILLING

COOKING TIME: 10 MINUTES

SERVES 4

225g (8oz) turkey mince
225g (8oz) herby sausagemeat
4 spring onions, trimmed and finely chopped
2 Tbsp tomato ketchup
$1/2$ red pepper, deseeded and finely chopped
Salt and pepper
1 mozzarella cheese, sliced
4 Tbsp oil

TO SERVE
4 burger buns, split and toasted
2 tsp mustard
2 tomatoes, sliced

1 In a bowl, mix together the turkey mince, sausagemeat, spring onions, ketchup, red pepper and seasoning.

2 Shape the mixture into eight thin burgers. Lay four burgers out in a row and place a cheese slice on top of each. Press the remaining burgers on top to enclose the cheese completely in a sort of sandwich. Chill for 2–3 hours to firm up.

3 Brush the burgers with the oil and cook on the grill rack for about 10 minutes until cooked through, turning over once.

4 Spread the bottom halves of the buns with the mustard and top with the burgers, tomato slices and bun lids.

Ciabatta stuffed with Parma ham and mozzarella

Bocconcini are tiny balls of mozzarella that can be bought in larger supermarkets and cheese shops. If your local store doesn't have them, use ordinary mozzarella and cut it up into bite-sized pieces.

PREPARATION TIME: 10 MINUTES

COOKING TIME: LESS THAN 10 MINUTES

SERVES 4

4 Tbsp olive oil
1 red pepper, quartered and deseeded
1 yellow pepper, quartered and deseeded
4 ciabatta rolls, split
2 tsp pesto
8 slices Parma ham
1 x 125g (4^1/$_2$ oz) tub bocconcini or mozzarella cheese cut into chunks
2 Tbsp chopped fresh parsley

1 Brush the peppers with half the olive oil and cook on the grill rack for about 5 minutes until tender but not scorched, turning them over once or twice.

2 Drizzle the cut sides of the ciabatta rolls with the remaining oil and lightly toast on the grill rack.

3 Spread the rolls with the pesto and fill with the peppers, Parma ham, mozzarella and parsley.

 ## tip

If you prefer, use wafer-thin slices of honey roast or other cooked ham instead of Parma ham. You could also wrap the prepared rolls in foil and return them to the grill rack for 10 minutes so the cheese melts.

Grilled aubergine and salami focaccia

Tapenade is a popular spread in Provence, where olive groves cover the sun-drenched hillsides. Made by pounding black olives with garlic, capers, anchovies, mustard and olive oil, it is delicious spread on toasted bread or canapés and can also be used as a stuffing for hard-boiled eggs. Look for jars of it in larger supermarket or buy it fresh from a deli counter.

PREPARATION TIME: 5 MINUTES

COOKING TIME: LESS THAN 10 MINUTES

SERVES 4

2 Tbsp olive oil
1 aubergine, cut into 5mm (¼in) slices
4 focaccia slices
4 tsp tapenade
115g (4oz) salami, thinly sliced
6 large basil leaves, torn

1 Brush the olive oil over the aubergine slices and cook on the grill rack for about 5 minutes or until golden.

2 Toast the focaccia slices lightly on the rack.

3 Spread the focaccia with the tapenade and top with the aubergine slices, salami and basil leaves.

tip

You'll find lots of different salami on your local deli counter including ones flavoured with garlic, whole peppercorns, fennel seeds, paprika and even red wine. If salami isn't to your taste, garlic sausage, Parma ham, mortadella or thin slices of another cooked meat could be used.

Plum lamb kebabs

Use lean lamb cut from the shoulder or leg and cut the meat into even-sized cubes so they cook evenly. The time given is for well-done meat so if you prefer your lamb rare, reduce the cooking time accordingly.

PREPARATION TIME: 15 MINUTES + MARINATING

COOKING TIME: 10 MINUTES

SERVES 4

450g (1lb) lean lamb, cut into 2.5cm (1in) cubes
1 tsp Thai red curry paste
1 tsp fresh garlic purée
2 Tbsp plum jam
1 Tbsp clear honey
Juice of 1 lime or 1/2 lemon

1 Spread out the lamb cubes in a shallow dish. Mix together the curry paste, garlic, plum jam, honey and lime or lemon juice and spoon over the lamb, turning the meat over until it's all coated.

2 Leave to marinate for 3–4 hours or until ready to cook.

3 Thread the lamb on to four skewers and cook on the grill rack for about 10 minutes, basting with any marinade left in the dish and turning the kebabs over once or twice.

tip

Finely chop any large pieces of fruit or leave them in the jar before mixing the plum jam with the other marinade ingredients. If you don't have plum, use apricot jam, orange chutney or hoi sin sauce instead.

Quarter pounders

Traditional burgers served with all the trimmings. Use best-quality steak mince and chill the burgers for several hours before cooking so they keep their shape on the grill.

PREPARATION TIME: 15 MINUTES + CHILLING

COOKING TIME: 10 MINUTES

SERVES 4

450g (1lb) lean steak mince
1 medium onion, peeled and minced or very finely chopped
75g (3oz) fresh breadcrumbs
1 tsp dried thyme
2 Tbsp tomato ketchup
Salt and pepper
1 medium egg, beaten
2 Tbsp oil

TO SERVE
Shredded lettuce
Dill pickle slices
Tomato slices
4 burger buns, split and toasted
Tomato pickle or mustard

1 Put the mince in a bowl and break up any lumps with a fork. Add the onion, breadcrumbs, thyme, ketchup and seasoning and mix well. Stir in the beaten egg so the mixture binds together.

2 With damp hands, shape the mixture into four burgers. Put on a plate and chill for at least 2 hours.

3 Brush the burgers with oil and cook on the grill rack for about 10 minutes, turning them over once, until well browned and cooked to your liking.

4 Layer the lettuce, burgers, dill pickle slices and tomato slices on the bottom of the buns. Add a spoonful of tomato pickle or mustard and top with the bun lids.

Hot-dog baguettes

A fun variation on one of our most popular fast foods: sausages for the adults, frankfurters for the kids.

PREPARATION TIME: 15 MINUTES

COOKING TIME: 20 MINUTES

SERVES 4

2 Tbsp oil
25g (1oz) butter
2 large onions, peeled and thinly sliced
1 Tbsp sugar
6 large sausages or thick frankfurters
4 half baguettes
4 Tbsp sweet pickle, chutney or sweet chilli sauce
4 Tbsp grated Cheddar cheese

TO SERVE
Mustard in a squeeze tube

1 Heat the oil and butter in a frying pan on a conventional hob and fry the onions for 10 minutes until softened and starting to brown, stirring frequently. Sprinkle over the sugar and continue to cook until the onions are golden and caramelized.

2 While the onions are cooking, cook the sausages on the chiminea grill rack until well browned and cooked through. If using frankfurters, they will only need 2–3 minutes on the grill to heat them through.

3 Cut each sausage or frankfurter into four slices on the diagonal. Cut the baguettes down the centre without cutting all the way through the bread, open up and toast the insides lightly on the grill rack.

4 Spread the insides of the baguettes with pickle, chutney or, for an extra kick, sweet chilli sauce. Spoon in the onions and tuck in the sausage slices.

5 Sit each hot dog in a foil case, squashing a sheet of foil around the baguette so the hot dogs sit upright and don't topple over. Sprinkle the cheese on top and place back on the grill rack until it melts. To serve, squeeze mustard over the top of each hot dog and serve at once.

Chicken fajitas

Cajun seasoning can be found among the spices in larger supermarkets, but substitute a mix of chilli powder and ground coriander if you prefer.

PREPARATION TIME: 20 MINUTES + MARINATING

COOKING TIME: 10 MINUTES

SERVES 4

3 boneless chicken breasts, skinned
2 tsp Cajun seasoning
1 tsp dried thyme
2 Tbsp oil
Juice of 1 lime
8 soft flour tortillas
2 Little Gem lettuces, shredded
2 large green chillies, deseeded and finely chopped
1 red onion, peeled and finely chopped
12 cherry tomatoes, halved

TO SERVE
Selection of relishes, eg:
   Guacamole (see page 153)
   Pepper, tomato and sweetcorn relish (see page 160)

1 Cut several slashes across each chicken breast and place them side by side in a shallow dish. Mix together the Cajun seasoning, dried thyme, oil and lime juice and spoon over the chicken, turning the breasts over until coated. Leave to marinate for 2–3 hours or until ready to cook.

2 Wrap the tortillas in foil and place on top of the chiminea to warm through.

3 Place the chicken breasts on the grill rack and cook for 5–8 minutes or until cooked all the way through, turning over halfway.

4 Slice the chicken into bite-sized pieces. Unwrap the tortillas and stack on a plate. Put the chicken, lettuce, chopped chillies, chopped onion and tomato halves on separate plates, along with bowls of relish. Leave people to fill their tortillas as they please.

2 party food

Chicken kebabs with orange and honey glaze
Sesame, ginger and soy beef
Sticky Chinese ribs
Thai-spiced prawns
Lamb, red onion and pepper sticks
Pork balls on skewers
Provençal stuffed focaccia
Roasted pepper, aubergine and Gorgonzola
   bruschetta
Prawn, pepper and pineapple skewers
Herby sausage patties
Sizzling mango chicken wings
Surf n' turf
Paella
Mustard-glazed brunch kebabs
Baked whole camembert
Greek chicken salad
Indonesian pork and chicken satay
Garlic butterfly prawns
Spicy grilled chicken thighs
Salmon and spinach burgers

Chicken kebabs with orange and honey glaze

The cooking time specified in this recipe is for average-sized chunks of chicken of about 2cm (¾in) but keep an eye on the kebabs so they don't overcook and dry out.

PREPARATION TIME: 15 MINUTES + MARINATING

COOKING TIME: 5–6 MINUTES

SERVES: 6

4 boneless chicken breasts or 8 boneless chicken thighs, skinned
    and cut into bite-size pieces
2 Tbsp clear honey
Finely grated rind and juice of 1 large orange
2 Tbsp Indonesian sweet soy sauce (kecap manis)
½ tsp ground turmeric
3 Tbsp sunflower oil
Freshly ground black pepper

TO SERVE
Flavoured mayonnaises (see page 150)
Spicy tomato sauce (see page 163)
Jacket potatoes (see page 141)

1 Put the chicken pieces into a bowl. Mix together the honey, orange rind, juice, soy sauce, turmeric, oil and black pepper and pour over the chicken, stirring until the pieces are well coated. Leave to marinate for 3–4 hours.

2 Thread the chicken pieces on to skewers and grill on the rack for 5–6 minutes or until cooked through, turning over once or twice and brushing with any marinade left in the bowl.

tip

If you prefer, thread the chicken pieces on to the skewers before marinating so it's one less job to organize before your guests arrive. If you don't want to serve the chicken still threaded on the skewers, serve with pitta bread split open and filled with salad, and the pieces of chicken arranged on top.

Sesame, ginger and soy beef

Serve these melt-in-the-mouth strips of beef wrapped in soft flour tortillas with salad and a spoonful of Spicy peanut dipping sauce, or wrapped in iceberg lettuce leaves with shredded carrot, spring onions and a bowl of soy sauce for dipping.

PREPARATION TIME: 15 MINUTES + MARINATING

COOKING TIME: ABOUT 5 MINUTES

SERVES: 6

700g (1lb 9oz) rump or sirloin steak, trimmed of fat
    and cut into thin strips
4 Tbsp dark soy sauce
2 tsp fresh garlic purée
2 tsp fresh ginger purée
1 tsp sesame oil
1 Tbsp soft brown sugar
2 Tbsp sesame seeds

TO SERVE
Soft tortillas, salad and Spicy Peanut dipping sauce (see page 157)
or Iceberg lettuce leaves, shredded carrot, spring onion and soy sauce

1 Spread out the steak strips in a shallow dish. Mix together the soy sauce, garlic purée, ginger purée, sesame oil and sugar and pour over the steak, turning the strips over until they are well coated. Leave to marinate for 4–5 hours or overnight.

2 Heat a cast-iron griddle or hot plate on the grill rack until very hot. Lift the steak from the dish and cook a few pieces at a time for about 1 minute or until done to your liking. The strips should be sticky and caramelized on the outside and tender inside.

3 Sprinkle with sesame seeds and serve.

tip

This marinade could also be used with lamb, pork and chicken or full-flavoured, oily fish such as salmon, mackerel or tuna.

Sticky Chinese ribs

The initial simmering of the ribs can be done well ahead in a large pan on a conventional hob and the ribs left to cool in their cooking liquid.

PREPARATION TIME 10 MINUTES + COOLING AND MARINATING

COOKING TIME 1 HOUR 5 MINUTES

SERVES 6

1.4kg (3lb) Chinese pork ribs
Approx. 600ml (1pt) chicken stock

GLAZE
1 tsp sesame oil
4 Tbsp dark soy sauce
4 garlic cloves, peeled and crushed
2 tsp fresh ginger purée
1 Tbsp clear honey
1 tsp chilli powder
2 Tbsp sesame seeds

1 Put the ribs into a deep roasting pan or large saucepan, cutting the sheets into shorter lengths if necessary, and pour over enough stock to just cover them.

2 Cover the pan tightly with foil or a lid and simmer the ribs on a conventional hob for 1 hour until tender. Remove from the heat and leave the ribs to cool in the stock.

3 Skim off any fat from the surface of the stock and lift out the ribs. (The stock can be saved as the base to make a gravy or sauce for another dish.)

4 Place the ribs in a dish. Mix together the sesame oil, soy sauce, garlic, ginger, honey and chilli powder and spread over the ribs, turning them over several times until they are well coated. Leave to marinate for 3–4 hours.

5 Grill the ribs on the rack for about 5 minutes until glistening and starting to scorch, turning them over once or twice, and brushing with any marinade left in the dish. Cut up into individual ribs and serve sprinkled with the sesame seeds.

Thai-spiced prawns

These tasty prawns can be served as a main course or as an appetizer with drinks.

PREPARATION TIME: 15 MINUTES + MARINATING

COOKING TIME: 5 MINUTES

SERVES 6

900g (2lb) raw tiger prawns, peeled, with tails left on
1 tsp lemon grass purée
1 tsp fresh ginger purée
1 tsp fresh garlic purée
2 Tbsp Thai fish sauce (nam pla)
3 Tbsp light soy sauce
1 tsp brown sugar
1 red chilli, deseeded and very finely chopped
½ lime

TO SERVE
Sweet chilli dipping sauce (see page 151)
Spicy peanut dipping sauce (see page 157)

1 Put the prawns in a bowl. Mix together the lemon grass, ginger, garlic, fish sauce, soy sauce, sugar and chilli, stirring until the sugar dissolves.

2 Pour the mixture over the prawns, turning them over so they are well coated. Leave to marinate for 30 minutes.

3 Thread the prawns on to skewers and cook on the grill rack for about 5 minutes or until the prawns turn pink and opaque. Squeeze over the lime juice and serve at once, with the dipping sauces.

 ## tip

If serving as an appetizer, push the prawns off the skewers on to a serving platter as soon as they are cooked and hand round with a pot of cocktail sticks for guests to spear individual prawns and dunk them in sweet chilli dipping sauce or spicy peanut dipping sauce.

Lamb, red onion and pepper sticks

If you use a thick, highly-concentrated balsamic vinegar for the marinade, reduce the amount specified in this recipe by half or dilute it with white wine or cider vinegar so that it doesn't overpower the other ingredients.

PREPARATION TIME: 15 MINUTES + MARINATING

COOKING TIME: LESS THAN 10 MINUTES

SERVES 8

1.4kg (3lb) lean lamb, cut into 2.5cm (1in) cubes
2 Tbsp ground coriander
1 Tbsp thyme leaves
2 Tbsp finely chopped rosemary leaves
4 Tbsp olive oil
2 Tbsp balsamic vinegar
Freshly ground black pepper
2 red onions, peeled, cut into wedges and layers separated
2 green peppers, deseeded and cut into 2.5cm (1in) chunks

1 Put the lamb in a bowl. Mix together the coriander, thyme, rosemary, olive oil and vinegar and season with plenty of black pepper. Pour this mixture over the lamb, turning the cubes over so they are well coated. Leave to marinate for 3–4 hours.

2 Thread the lamb, red onion pieces and pepper chunks on to eight large or 16 small skewers and grill on the rack for 7–8 minutes, turning them over regularly.

 ## tip

If you have rosemary growing in your garden, cut some long sprigs and strip the leaves – which you will use in the marinade (step 1) – from the stalks, leaving just a few at the tip. Shave the cut ends of the stalks to a point and you can then use the aromatic stalks as skewers. As rosemary leaves are quite tough, chop them very finely before adding to the marinade.

Pork balls on skewers

Another good accompaniment for these tasty meatballs would be a refreshing salad of sliced tomatoes, finely chopped red onion and black olives.

PREPARATION TIME: 30 MINUTES + CHILLING

COOKING TIME: 20 MINUTES

SERVES: 8

1kg (2¼ lb) pork mince
1 Tbsp finely chopped fresh mint
1 Tbsp finely chopped fresh sage
1 tsp smoked paprika
1 Tbsp ground coriander
115g (4oz) fresh breadcrumbs
Freshly ground black pepper
2 eggs, beaten
Plain flour for dusting
Olive oil for brushing

TO SERVE
Chickpea tabbouleh (see page 142)
Tzatziki (see page 158)

1 In a large bowl, mix together the pork, mint, sage, smoked paprika, coriander, breadcrumbs and pepper.

2 Stir in the beaten eggs to bind the mixture together and, with floured hands, shape the mixture into 24 small balls. Thread on to skewers and chill for 3–4 hours.

3 Brush the pork balls all over with olive oil and grill on the rack or on a hot plate for about 20 minutes until cooked through, turning them over occasionally so they are evenly browned.

 ## tip

If you're worried the pork balls will break up on the grill rack, cook them on a lightly greased hot plate instead. Chill the balls for several hours before cooking so they have plenty of time to firm up.

Provençal stuffed focaccia

More interesting than plain garlic bread, the focaccia can be prepared ahead of your party and wrapped in foil ready to be heated as and when required. French sticks would make a crusty alternative to focaccia.

PREPARATION TIME: 15 MINUTES + COOLING

COOKING TIME: 30 MINUTES

SERVES 6

1 focaccia
2 Tbsp olive oil
1 red onion, peeled and finely chopped
1 red pepper, deseeded and finely chopped
1 courgette, finely chopped
2 tsp finely chopped fresh thyme or rosemary
2 Tbsp grated Parmesan cheese
150g (5oz) Gruyère cheese, finely diced
Freshly ground black pepper

1 Cut the focaccia in half horizontally and hollow out the two halves, removing as much of the crumb as possible but without splitting the crust.

2 Heat the oil in a pan on a conventional hob and fry the onion, red pepper, courgette and thyme or rosemary for about 10 minutes until soft but not brown. Leave to cool, then stir in the Parmesan and Gruyère and season with plenty of black pepper.

3 Spoon the vegetables and cheese into the bottom half of the focaccia, packing the mixture in tightly, and replace the 'lid' – the top half of the focaccia.

4 Wrap the focaccia in foil, sealing the edges tightly, and place on the grill rack for about 15 minutes, until piping hot and the cheese has melted. Open the foil and cut into wedges to serve.

 ## tip

The crumb from the hollowed-out bread can be kept for use in another recipe such as crumbs for coating fish cakes (see page 27) or sprinkling over a gratin. Reduce the pieces of bread to coarse crumbs in a food processor and freeze in a tightly sealed plastic bag if not using within 1–2 days.

Roasted pepper, aubergine and Gorgonzola bruschetta

There's always a lively debate as to whether aubergine slices should be salted and left to 'degorge' before cooking. The 'no' camp say it's unnecessary as bitter juices have been bred out of modern varieties; the 'yes' camp argue the flesh will absorb less oil as it cooks, so the choice is yours…

PREPARATION TIME: 15 MINUTES + COOLING

COOKING TIME: ABOUT 20 MINUTES

MAKES 6

3 red peppers
1 aubergine, cut into 5mm (¼in) slices
Extra virgin olive oil for brushing
6 slices country bread or ciabatta
3 fat garlic cloves, peeled and halved lengthways
250g (9oz) Gorgonzola cheese, crumbled or cubed
Freshly ground black pepper
Torn basil leaves to garnish

1 Grill the peppers on the rack for about 10 minutes or until the skins are blistered and scorched all over. Wrap them in foil and leave until cool enough to handle.

2 While the peppers are cooling, brush the aubergine slices with olive oil and grill on the rack for about 5 minutes until golden and tender, turning over once.

3 Unwrap the foil, strip off the pepper skins, halve, remove the seeds and cut the flesh into thick strips.

4 Toast the bread slices lightly on both sides on the rack, and rub with the cut sides of the garlic cloves.

5 Drizzle the bread with a little olive oil and pile on the roasted vegetables and cheese. Grind over plenty of black pepper. Warm the bruschettas near the oven, or in a shallow baking tray on top of the chiminea until the cheese begins to melt. Serve at once, garnished with torn basil leaves.

 ## tip

Baguette slices are a little small for these bruschettas, so use good-sized slices of country bread or ciabatta so the vegetables and cheese don't topple off the sides.

Prawn, pepper and pineapple skewers

Serve these with a small dish of soy sauce or plum sauce for dipping. The skewers can also be accompanied with egg fried rice or egg noodles tossed with chilli sauce, soy and finely chopped stir-fried vegetables for a more substantial meal.

PREPARATION TIME: 10 MINUTES + MARINATING

COOKING TIME: 5 MINUTES

MAKES 8

700g (1lb 9oz) raw tiger prawns, peeled
2 Tbsp light soy sauce
1 Tbsp lime juice
1 tsp clear honey
1 tsp sweet chilli sauce
2 green peppers, deseeded and cut into chunks
4 pineapple rings, cut into chunks

1 Put the prawns in a dish. Mix together the soy sauce, lime juice, honey and chilli sauce and pour over the prawns, turning them over until coated. Leave to marinate for 30 minutes.

2 Thread the prawns, pepper chunks and pineapple pieces alternately on to eight skewers. Cook on the grill rack for about 5 minutes or until the prawns are pink and opaque, brushing with any marinade left in the dish and turning over once.

tip

Use either fresh or tinned pineapple, cutting the rings into similar sized pieces to the green pepper.

Herby sausage patties

The patties can be served like burgers in small toasted buns or on their own with a couple of contrasting dips such as tomato ketchup and wholegrain mustard.

PREPARATION TIME: 20 MINUTES + CHILLING

COOKING TIME: 10–15 MINUTES

SERVES 6

900g (2lb) sausagemeat
2 tsp chopped fresh thyme
2 Tbsp chopped fresh parsley
2 Tbsp tomato pickle
2 Tbsp Worcestershire sauce
4 Tbsp plain flour
Oil for brushing

1 Break up the sausagemeat in the bowl. Add the herbs, tomato pickle and Worcestershire sauce and mix well.

2 Shape the mixture into 18 flat cakes and dust with flour. Chill for 1 hour or until ready to cook.

3 Brush the patties with oil and grill on the rack for 10–15 minutes until golden brown and cooked through, turning over once.

Sizzling mango chicken wings

The tips or pinions of chicken wings have no meat on them and are frequently overlooked by plucking machines, so it makes sense to snip them off with kitchen scissors before cooking. Trimming off the tips also stops them burning on the rack and gives the wings a neater shape.

PREPARATION TIME: 10 MINUTES + MARINATING

COOKING TIME: 15 MINUTES

SERVES 6

12 large chicken wings
4 Tbsp mango chutney, with any large pieces of fruit removed
   or finely chopped
1 tsp ground cumin
4 Tbsp coconut milk

1 Spread out the chicken wings in a shallow dish. Mix together the chutney, cumin and coconut milk and spoon over the chicken until coated. Leave to marinate for 3–4 hours or until ready to cook.

2 Grill the chicken wings on the rack for about 15 minutes until golden brown and cooked through, turning them over once or twice and basting with any leftover marinade.

tip

Other chicken joints such as thighs, legs or drumsticks can be cooked in the same way but the cooking time will need to be increased or the joints pre-cooked and then just glazed and finished off on the chiminea. To test if chicken is cooked, push a skewer into the thickest part of the meat. It should feel tender and the juices should run clear.

Surf 'n' turf

A barbecue special from Down Under, where cooking outdoors is a way of life. This recipe is just as easily cooked in a chiminea as on a more conventional Aussie barbecue.

PREPARATION TIME: 15 MINUTES + MARINATING

COOKING TIME: 5 MINUTES

SERVES 6

3 Tbsp dark soy sauce
3 Tbsp lime juice
3 Tbsp oil
1 Tbsp maple syrup
1 tsp dried mixed herbs
6 rump or sirloin steaks, trimmed of fat
12–18 large raw prawns, with heads and tails left on

1 Whisk together the soy sauce, lime juice, oil, maple syrup and dried herbs.

2 Put the steaks in a single layer in a shallow dish. Peel the shells off the prawns, leaving the heads and tails on, devein and spread out in another dish.

3 Pour half the soy-sauce mixture over the steaks and leave to marinate for 3–4 hours. Pour the rest of the marinade over the prawns 1 hour before you are ready to start cooking.

4 Lift the steaks and prawns from their marinades and grill on the rack, turning over once and brushing with any remaining marinade. The steaks will take about 2–3 minutes on each side for medium and the prawns 2–3 minutes in total.

Paella

You'll need a special paella pan, wok or large frying pan to cook this dish on top of the chiminea. Serve it straight from the pan with just a simple green salad as accompaniment.

PREPARATION TIME: 20 MINUTES

COOKING TIME: 45–50 MINUTES

SERVES 6

2 Tbsp olive oil
1 large Spanish onion, peeled and thinly sliced
1 red pepper, deseeded and chopped
1 green pepper, deseeded and chopped
115g (4oz) chorizo sausage, chopped
1 boneless chicken breast, skinned and cut into small pieces
350g (12oz) paella rice
150ml (5fl oz) dry white wine
425ml (15fl oz) fish stock
Pinch saffron threads, soaked in 2 Tbsp warm water for 5 minutes
115g (4oz) frozen peas
250g (9oz) raw tiger prawns, peeled
150g (5oz) squid, cut into rings
500g (1lb 2oz) mussels, in their shells

1 Heat the oil in a paella pan, wok or large frying pan on top of the chiminea, add the onion and fry for 5 minutes.

2 Add the peppers and chorizo and cook for a further 5 minutes, stirring frequently.

3 Stir in the chicken and rice and add the wine, stock and saffron threads with their soaking liquid. Stir well and cook for 20–25 minutes or until the rice is almost tender.

4 Add the peas, prawns and squid and tuck the mussels in amongst the other ingredients. Cook for a further 10 minutes until the prawns turn pink, the rice is cooked and the mussels have opened (discard any that stay tightly closed).

Mustard-glazed brunch kebabs

These can be served with scrambled eggs cooked on a conventional hob or on top of the chiminea.

PREPARATION TIME: 20 MINUTES + MARINATING

COOKING TIME: 10–15 MINUTES

SERVES 8

8 lamb's kidneys
8 rashers streaky bacon, halved
16 cocktail sausages
16 small-cup mushrooms
1 red pepper, deseeded and cut into 2.5cm (1in) chunks
16 small new potatoes, cooked
1 Tbsp Dijon mustard
1 tsp clear honey
2 Tbsp oil
4 Tbsp orange juice

TO SERVE
Split and toasted bagels

1 Cut the kidneys in half and snip out the cores with kitchen scissors. Stretch the halved bacon rashers with the back of a knife and roll up.

2 Thread the kidneys, bacon rolls, sausages, mushrooms, red pepper and potatoes alternately on to eight large or 16 small skewers and place side by side in a shallow dish.

3 Whisk together the mustard, honey, oil and orange juice and brush over the kebabs. Leave to marinate for 1 hour or longer before cooking.

4 Grill the kebabs on the rack for 10–15 minutes or until cooked, turning them over once or twice and basting or brushing with any marinade left in the dish. Serve with split and toasted bagels.

 ## tip

Ensure the pieces of food are of similar size so everything cooks evenly.

Baked whole camembert

It's important to look for a camembert packed in a wooden rather than a cardboard box, and don't forget to remove the inner waxed paper wrapper before baking. The box can either be wrapped in foil and placed directly on the rack or stood, unwrapped, on a baking sheet.

PREPARATION TIME: 5 MINUTES

COOKING TIME: 20 MINUTES

SERVES 4

1 whole firm camembert cheese in a wooden box
2 bay leaves

TO SERVE
Crusty bread
Crudités, such as carrot sticks, small radishes and pepper wedges

1 Remove the camembert from its box and discard the inner wrapper. Return the cheese to the box and lay the bay leaves on top.

2 Replace the lid and stand the box on a piece of foil, scrunching the foil around the bottom of the box to protect it from any flames from the coals that could singe or set it alight.

3 Bake on the grill rack for about 20 minutes or until the camembert is bubbling. Discard the lid of the box and the bay leaves and serve it hot straight from the box.

Greek chicken salad

Long, oval kalamata olives from Greece have a full flavour and soft, juicy texture, making them ideal for salads. Look for the ones preserved in olive oil rather than brine.

PREPARATION TIME: 20 MINUTES + COOLING

COOKING TIME: 10–15 MINUTES

SERVES 8

4 chicken breasts, skin on
8 Tbsp olive oil
2 Tbsp tarragon vinegar or white wine vinegar
2 tsp wholegrain mustard
Salt and freshly ground black pepper
150g (5oz) rocket leaves
275g (10oz) feta cheese, crumbled
16 cherry tomatoes, halved
½ cucumber, thinly sliced
225g (8oz) green seedless grapes
175g (6oz) black kalamata olives
2 Tbsp snipped fresh chives

1 Brush the chicken breasts with 2 Tbsp of the oil and grill on the rack for 10–15 minutes or until cooked through, turning them over halfway. Cut into thin slices across the grain of the meat, removing the skin first if you're not going to eat it. (It's still a good idea to cook the breasts with the skin on, however, since this keeps the meat moist.)

2 In a bowl, whisk together the remaining olive oil, vinegar, mustard and seasoning. Add the hot chicken slices and leave them to cool in the dressing.

3 Line a serving dish with the rocket and top with the crumbled feta, cherry tomato halves, sliced cucumber, grapes and olives. Spoon over the chicken and any dressing remaining in the bowl then sprinkle with the chives.

tip

As the chicken cools in the dressing (step 2) it will absorb the flavours from the dressing and become deliciously tender and succulent.

Indonesian pork and chicken satay

A popular street snack in South East Asia, these tasty skewers make great finger food for a party. Serve them with spicy peanut dipping sauce.

PREPARATION TIME: 15 MINUTES + MARINATING

COOKING TIME: LESS THAN 5 MINUTES

SERVES 8

2 garlic cloves, peeled and crushed
4 Tbsp Indonesian sweet soy sauce (kecap manis) or dark soy sauce
Juice of 2 limes
1 tsp sweet chilli sauce
1 tsp fresh ginger purée
2 boneless chicken breasts, skinned and cut into thin strips
250g (9oz) pork escalopes, cut into thin strips

TO SERVE
Spicy peanut dipping sauce (see page 157)

1 Whisk the garlic, soy sauce, lime juice, sweet chilli sauce and ginger purée together in a dish until combined. Add the chicken and pork strips, turning the meat over until well coated. Leave to marinate for 3–4 hours or until ready to cook.

2 Thread the chicken and pork on to separate skewers and grill on the rack for 3–4 minutes. Turn them over halfway and baste with any marinade left in the dish, until the meat is well browned and cooked through.

tip

Indonesian soy sauce, known as kecap manis, is thicker and more syrupy than Chinese or Japanese soy sauces and has a rich, dark flavour. Bottles of it can be found in Asian food stores and major supermarkets and it is worth seeking out as the sugar in the sauce helps to caramelize the meat as it cooks.

Garlic butterfly prawns

Cook these in two batches in a wok on top of the chiminea, then tip on to a platter and serve with a couple of contrasting dips such as garlic and lemon mayonnaise and spicy tomato sauce.

PREPARATION TIME: 10 MINUTES + MARINATING

COOKING TIME: LESS THAN 10 MINUTES

SERVES 8

900g (2lb) raw king prawns
4 garlic cloves, peeled and crushed
Juice of 1 lemon
4 Tbsp extra virgin olive oil
Freshly ground black pepper
3 Tbsp chopped flat-leaf parsley

TO SERVE
Garlic and lemon mayonnaise (see page 150)
Spicy tomato sauce (see page 153)

1 Remove the heads from the prawns and peel off the shells, but leave the tails on.

2 Using a sharp knife, cut down the back of each prawn, without cutting all the way through, and pull out the black thread running down it.

3 In a bowl, whisk together the garlic, lemon juice and half the olive oil. Season with plenty of freshly ground black pepper and add the prawns, tossing them until well coated. Leave to marinate for 15 minutes.

4 Heat the remaining olive oil in a wok on top of the chiminea, add half the prawns and some of their marinade and stir-fry for 2–3 minutes until they turn pink. Remove from the wok and place on a serving plate, then stir-fry the remaining prawns in the same way.

5 Scatter over the parsley and serve the prawns hot, with the dips.

Spicy grilled chicken thighs

As thighs are quite small, it's worth threading them on to long skewers when you're cooking a batch for a party so you don't have too many joints to turn over. Prepare the chicken the day before and leave it to marinate overnight so it has time to absorb all the spicy flavours.

PREPARATION TIME: 15 MINUTES + MARINATING

COOKING TIME: 35 MINUTES

SERVES 8

16 chicken thighs

MARINADE
3 Tbsp oil
2 large onions, peeled and chopped
1 Tbsp chilli powder
1 Tbsp ground coriander
2.5cm (1in) piece root ginger, peeled and chopped
4 garlic cloves, peeled and chopped
Juice of 1 lemon
200g (7oz) natural yogurt
1 tsp salt

1 Place the chicken thighs in a single layer in a shallow dish.

2 To make the marinade, heat the oil in a pan, add the onions and cook over a gentle heat for about 15 minutes until the onions are soft but not browned. Add the chilli powder and coriander and cook for 5 minutes, stirring occasionally. Leave to cool.

3 Tip the onion mixture into a food processor, add the remaining marinade ingredients and blend until smooth. Spread over the chicken thighs until well coated and leave to marinate for several hours or overnight.

4 Thread the thighs on to long metal skewers and grill on the rack for 15 minutes or until cooked through, turning regularly.

Salmon and spinach burgers

Before mincing the salmon for this novel variation on the more typical barbecue burger, check the fish for any small rib bones by running your finger down the thickest part of the flesh, and pull these out with tweezers.

PREPARATION TIME: 20 MINUTES + MARINATING

COOKING TIME: LESS THAN 10 MINUTES

SERVES 4

450g (1lb) salmon fillet, skinned
115g (4oz) baby spinach leaves, roughly chopped
Finely grated rind of 1 lemon
2 Tbsp mayonnaise
Salt and pepper
Plain flour for dusting
1 egg, beaten
75g (3oz) dry or fresh breadcrumbs
Sunflower oil for brushing
4 burger buns, split and toasted
Lettuce leaves, tomato slices, cucumber slices
Pepper, tomato and sweetcorn relish (see page 160)

1 Cut the salmon into small pieces. Place the fish in a food processor with the chopped spinach and blend until coarsely minced, taking care not to over-process and reduce the mixture to a paste. Transfer to a bowl and stir in the lemon rind, mayonnaise and seasoning.

2 Divide the mixture into four and shape into burgers. Dust them with flour, brush with beaten egg and press over the breadcrumbs until evenly coated. Chill for 1 hour or until ready to cook.

3 Brush the burgers with oil on both sides. Grill directly on the rack or on a cast-iron griddle or frying pan on the rack for 3–4 minutes on each side until golden brown.

4 Layer the bottom halves of the buns with lettuce, tomato slices, a salmon burger and cucumber slices. Top with a spoonful of relish and press on the bun lids.

3 main courses – fish

Blackened salmon
Trout, fennel and tomato parcels
Chilli squid with garlic and lemon
Tuna and coriander cakes
Teriyaki roast salmon
Devilled mackerel
Tomato and orange-glazed swordfish skewers
Parma ham-wrapped monkfish and scallop
  kebabs
White fish hot pot
Tuna with an oyster sauce and chilli glaze
Sea bass with Asian greens
Baked prawns with feta
Spiced tuna with grilled vegetables and warm
  mustard vinaigrette
Steamed monkfish and prawns with banana
  leaves
King prawns with chermoula

Blackened salmon

Blackening is not a sly ruse to pass off burnt offerings as fine dining, but an aromatic way of cooking fish and meat that's popular in America's Deep South. The food is coated in a mixture of herbs, garlic and spices and then left to marinate.

PREPARATION TIME: 15 MINUTES + STANDING

COOKING TIME: 10 MINUTES

SERVES 4

2 Tbsp dried mixed herbs
2 tsp smoked paprika
2 garlic cloves, skinned and crushed
1 tsp fresh ginger purée
2 tsp coriander seeds, crushed
4 Tbsp lime or lemon juice
½ tsp freshly ground black pepper
4 x 175g (6oz) salmon fillets
2 Tbsp oil
50g (2oz) butter

TO SERVE
Avocado, pineapple and kidney bean salsa (see page 161)

1 To make the blackening mix, stir together the dried herbs, smoked paprika, garlic, ginger, crushed coriander seeds, half the lime or lemon juice and the pepper.

2 Place the salmon fillets, skin side down, in a single layer in a shallow dish and spread the blackening mix over them. Set aside for 1 hour.

3 Heat the oil in a cast-iron frying pan or griddle on the rack and fry the salmon fillets, blackening mix down, for 5 minutes. Turn the fillets over and cook for a further 3–5 minutes or until done. The time taken will depend on the thickness of the fish.

4 Remove the salmon from the pan to serving plates. Add the butter and the remaining lime or lemon juice to the pan and heat until the butter melts and foams. Spoon the juices over the fish and serve with the salsa.

Trout, fennel and tomato parcels

Trout and fennel are natural partners, as the delicate aniseed flavour of the fennel complements fish perfectly. Cooking them together in a tightly sealed foil parcel traps all the aroma inside and prevents the fish drying out.

PREPARATION TIME: 10 MINUTES

COOKING TIME: 10 MINUTES

SERVES 4

1 large fennel bulb, thinly sliced
4 plum tomatoes, quartered
150g (5oz) brown cap mushrooms, sliced or quartered
4 trout, cleaned
4 Tbsp Pernod, Ricard or ouzo
4 Tbsp olive oil
Freshly ground black pepper

TO SERVE
New potato salad with bacon, rocket and spring onions
  (see page 143)

1 Cut four sheets of foil, each one large enough to enclose a trout. Place the sheets on the worktop and divide the sliced fennel, quartered tomatoes and sliced mushrooms between them.

2 Lay the trout on top, gather the foil around and spoon over the Pernod, Ricard or ouzo and olive oil. Season with freshly ground black pepper and wrap the foil around the vegetables and fish, folding over the edges to make tightly sealed parcels.

3 Place the parcels on the grill rack and cook for 10 minutes or until the trout flesh flakes easily. Serve with warm new potato salad .

 ## tip

Only slice the fennel just before cooking or it will start to oxidize and turn brown. If you do need to prepare it in advance, keep the slices in a bowl of cold water with a tablespoon of lemon juice added, or toss the slices with lemon juice and store in a tightly-sealed plastic bag.

Chilli squid with garlic and lemon

Most squid are sold ready-prepared but if the ones you buy aren't, this is simple to do. Start by holding the body of the squid and pulling out the head and white intestines in one go. Cut off the tentacles and reserve, discarding the rest. Pull the clear, plastic-like quill out of the body and discard. Rub off the thin, brown skin, rinse the body and tentacles and the squid is ready to cook.

PREPARATION TIME: 10 MINUTES + COOLING

COOKING TIME: LESS THAN 5 MINUTES

SERVES 4

100ml (4fl oz) extra virgin olive oil
Finely grated rind and juice of 1 large or 2 small lemons
2 garlic cloves, peeled and crushed
1 red chilli, deseeded and very finely chopped
2 Tbsp chopped fresh parsley
1 shallot, peeled and finely chopped
Freshly ground black pepper
600g (1lb 5 oz) prepared squid

TO SERVE
Green or mixed salad
Crusty bread

1 In a bowl, whisk together the olive oil, lemon rind and juice, garlic, chopped chilli, parsley and shallot and season with freshly ground black pepper.

2 Grill the squid on the rack or on a hot plate for about 1 minute or until they are opaque. Remove to a board, slice into rings and add to the oil and lemon mixture while still warm.

3 Leave to cool before serving with salad and chunks of crusty bread to mop up the juices.

Tuna and coriander cakes

This recipe requires dry breadcrumbs. You can make your own by spreading fresh crumbs out on a tray and leaving them for 2-3 days, turning the crumbs over occasionally. Once dry, store the crumbs in a tightly sealed jar.

PREPARATION TIME: 20 MINUTES + CHILLING

COOKING TIME: 10 MINUTES

SERVES 4

450g (1lb) potatoes, boiled and mashed
1 x 400g (14oz) tin tuna, drained and flaked
2 spring onions, trimmed and finely chopped
2 Tbsp chopped fresh coriander
Salt and pepper
4 Tbsp plain flour
2 eggs, beaten
75g (3oz) fresh or dry breadcrumbs
2 Tbsp oil
50g (2oz) butter

1 In a bowl, mix together the potatoes, tuna, spring onions, coriander and seasoning until evenly combined.

2 Divide the mixture into eight and shape into round flat cakes. Dust with flour, brush with beaten egg and press in the crumbs until well coated. Chill for 1 hour or until ready to cook.

3 Heat the oil and butter together until the butter melts, brush over the tuna cakes and grill on the rack for 10 minutes until golden brown, or cook on a hot plate or griddle, turning over once and brushing with any leftover oil and butter.

 ## tip

These fish cakes could be made with tinned salmon instead of tuna, or cooked flaked fresh fish such as mackerel, salmon, trout or smoked haddock. (It doesn't matter if the tinned fish has been tinned in oil or water.) Different herbs can also be added – parsley, tarragon, chives, chervil or a mix of fresh herbs would all work well.

Teriyaki roast salmon

Teriyaki is a mix of Japanese soy sauce, mirin, sake and sugar, which cooks to a sweet, shiny glaze on chicken, meat or fish. The glaze works particularly well with salmon, as it complements the rich oily flesh of the fish perfectly.

PREPARATION TIME: 10 MINUTES + PLUS MARINATING

COOKING TIME: LESS THAN 10 MINUTES

SERVES 4

4 x 175g (6oz) salmon fillets
4 Tbsp Japanese soy sauce
4 Tbsp mirin
2 Tbsp sake
1 Tbsp soft brown sugar

TO SERVE
1/2 daikon (white radish), peeled and cut into matchsticks
1 large carrot, cut into matchsticks
4 spring onions, shredded

1 Place the salmon, skin side down, in a shallow dish. Stir the soy sauce, mirin, sake and sugar together until the sugar dissolves and spoon over the fish. Leave to marinate for 1 hour.

2 Lift the salmon from the marinade and grill on the rack for 3–4 minutes on each side until done, brushing with any glaze left in the dish while it cooks. The exact cooking time will depend on the thickness of the fillets.

3 For a Japanese accompaniment, serve with a crisp salad of daikon (white radish), carrot and spring onions.

tip

Teriyaki sauce can be bought ready-made, which is fine if you don't want to buy mirin and sake to make your own. The teriyaki mix could also be used to glaze other types of fish such as cod, haddock or tuna. You could also use it for chicken.

Devilled mackerel

The 'devil' mix would work well with other oily fish such as tuna or herrings, although cooking times will vary according to the thickness of the fish, and whether it is on or off the bone.

PREPARATION TIME: 5 MINUTES + MARINATING

COOKING TIME: LESS THAN 10 MINUTES

SERVES 4

4 whole mackerel, cleaned
1 Tbsp paprika
1 tsp ground coriander
1 Tbsp Worcestershire sauce
3 Tbsp white wine vinegar
1 tsp English mustard powder
1 lemon, cut into 8 wedges

TO SERVE
Layered summer salad (see page 143)
Jacket potatoes (see page 141) and Coleslaw (see page 140)

1 Slash the skin of the mackerel several times on each side and lay them side by side in a shallow dish. Whisk together the paprika, coriander, Worcestershire sauce, vinegar and mustard powder and spoon over the fish. Turn over and leave to marinate for 1 hour.

2 Grill the mackerel on the rack for about 5 minutes on each side or until cooked. Squeeze the lemon wedges over the fish and serve at once.

 ## tip

The mix can also be used with fish fillets if you prefer. Leave the skin on the fillets, scoring it lightly several times with a sharp knife. Marinate and cook in the same way as for whole fish, adjusting the cooking time if necessary.

Tomato and orange-glazed swordfish skewers

Swordfish is perfect for kebabs as its firm flesh is tasty and doesn't fall apart when cooked.

PREPARATION TIME: 10 MINUTES + MARINATING

COOKING TIME: 5 MINUTES

SERVES 4

450g (1lb) swordfish steaks, skinned
Juice of 1 orange
1 tsp fresh ginger purée
1 Tbsp oil
2 Tbsp tomato ketchup
1 Tbsp chopped fresh mint
1 tsp maple syrup or clear honey

TO SERVE
Calypso rice salad (see page 147)

1 Cut the swordfish into thin strips about 2 cm (3/4 in) wide and thread on to skewers in a concertina fashion rather than rolling them.

2 Place the skewers side by side in a shallow dish. Whisk together the orange juice, ginger purée, oil, ketchup, mint and maple syrup or honey and spoon over the fish. Leave to marinate for 1 hour.

3 Grill the skewers on the rack for about 5 minutes until the fish is opaque, turning them over once or twice and basting or brushing with any marinade left in the dish.

tip

Monkfish is another firm fish that's ideal for kebabs
and could be used for this recipe. You could also
alternate the chunks of swordfish with tiger prawns.

Parma ham-wrapped monkfish and scallop kebabs

If the scallops still have their orange roes attached, these can be left on or removed as you prefer.

PREPARATION TIME: 15 MINUTES + MARINATING

COOKING TIME: LESS THAN 10 MINUTES

SERVES 4

8 large scallops, corals on or removed as preferred
450g (1lb) monkfish fillet, skinned and cut into 2.5cm (1in) chunks
2 Tbsp light olive oil
Juice of 1/2 lemon
1 tsp clear honey
1 garlic clove, peeled and crushed
1 tsp dried or fresh thyme
75g (3oz) thin slices Parma ham

1 Put the scallops and chunks of monkfish in a bowl. Whisk together the olive oil, lemon juice, honey, garlic and thyme and pour over. Leave to marinate for 1 hour.

2 Drain the scallops and monkfish and wrap the monkfish in the Parma ham, snipping the slices into smaller pieces with kitchen scissors as necessary.

3 Thread the scallops and Parma ham-wrapped monkfish alternately on to four skewers and grill on the rack for 5–6 minutes. Turn the skewers over once or twice and baste with any marinade left in the bowl, until the ham is crisp and the monkfish and scallops opaque.

tip

Trim off the fat from the ham and any thin skin from
the monkfish before you assemble the kebabs.

White fish hot pot

Cook this in a wok or heavy pan, uncovered, on top of the chiminea or in a flameproof casserole with a lid on the rack.

PREPARATION TIME 20 MINUTES

COOKING TIME 25 MINUTES

SERVES 4

2 Tbsp olive oil
1 red onion, peeled and thinly sliced
1 courgette, sliced
1 red pepper, deseeded and chopped
115g (4oz) mushrooms, sliced
1 tsp dried oregano
1 glass dry white wine
300ml (10fl oz) fish stock
2 Tbsp sun-dried tomato purée
1 x 400g (14oz) tin chopped tomatoes
1 x 400g (14oz) tin flageolet beans, drained and rinsed
700g (1lb 9oz) cod, monkfish or other white fish fillet, skinned and cut
    into 2.5cm (1in) chunks
Salt and pepper

TO SERVE
Hot garlic bread

1 Heat the oil in a large pan, or a wok on top of the chimInea, add the union and fry for 5 minutes, Add the courgette, red pepper, mushrooms and oregano and fry for a further 5 minutes.

2 Pour in the wine and bubble for 2–3 minutes before adding the stock, tomato purée and chopped tomatoes.

3 Stir until the mixture comes to a simmer, and add in the beans. If you want to use a casserole dish on the rack, now transfer the contents of the large pan into the casserole, cover and move it down onto the rack. Cook for 5 minutes before adding the fish. Season to taste, then simmer for a further 5 minutes or until the fish turns opaque. Serve with hot garlic bread.

Tuna with an oyster sauce and chilli glaze

Made from ground oysters, water, salt, cornflour and caramel, Chinese oyster sauce is available from most supermarkets. Once opened, the bottle needs to be kept in the fridge or the sauce will go mouldy.

PREPARATION TIME: 10 MINUTES + MARINATING

COOKING TIME: LESS THAN 10 MINUTES

SERVES 4

1 tsp fresh ginger purée
6 Tbsp oyster sauce
2 tsp sweet chilli sauce
Juice of $^1/_2$ lemon
4 x 175g (6oz) tuna steaks

TO SERVE
Avocado, pineapple and kidney bean salsa (see page 161)

1 In a shallow dish, whisk together the ginger purée, oyster sauce, chilli sauce and lemon juice until combined. Add the tuna, turning the fillets over until they are well coated. Leave to marinate for 30 minutes.

2 Heat a heavy griddle or cast-iron frying pan on the grill rack, add the tuna and cook for 3–4 minutes on each side, depending on how well you like your fish cooked and basting with any marinade left in the dish.

tip

Make sure the pan is really hot before you add the tuna or the fillets will stick.

Sea bass with Asian greens

Fillets or small whole fish can be used for this delicately flavoured Oriental recipe. Serve the fish with a mixed salad.

PREPARATION TIME: 10 MINUTES

COOKING TIME: LESS THAN 10 MINUTES

SERVES 4

4 x 175g (6oz) sea bass fillets or 4 small whole sea bass
Freshly ground black pepper
2 baby pak choy heads, halved lengthways
250g (9oz) tenderstem broccoli florets
50g (2oz) mange tout
2.5cm (1in) piece root ginger, peeled and cut into fine shreds
4 Tbsp rice wine
4 Tbsp light soy sauce

1 Season the fish with freshly ground black pepper. Cut four sheets of foil, each large enough to enclose a piece of fish comfortably, and place a fillet or whole fish in the centre of each.

2 Top with the pak choy, broccoli and mange tout, dividing the vegetables equally between the parcels. Add the ginger and drizzle over the rice wine and soy sauce.

3 Wrap the foil around the fish and vegetables, folding the edges over to make tightly sealed parcels.

4 Cook the parcels on the rack for 6 minutes for fillets and 7–8 minutes for whole fish or until the sea bass is cooked and the greens just tender.

tip

Chinese rice wine can be bought in Oriental stores and ranges from mild and fragrant to powerful and sherry-like. The stronger, sherry-like wine is used to flavour the fish so, if you don't want to buy a bottle specially, substitute dry sherry or a full-bodied white wine such as Chardonnay.

Baked prawns with feta

This is a speciality of seaside tavernas along the Athens to Sounion coast and is enjoyed by countless city dwellers and tourists escaping the relentless summer heat of the cities. Use large prawns and a well-flavoured tomato sauce, either bought or homemade.

PREPARATION TIME: 15 MINUTES

COOKING TIME: 20 MINUTES

SERVES 4

600ml (1pt) tomato sauce (see tip, below)
200g (7oz) feta cheese, crumbled
8 spring onions, trimmed and sliced
1 tsp fresh thyme leaves
1 Tbsp chopped fresh oregano
16 large raw prawns, peeled
4 Tbsp ouzo, brandy or dry white wine
Freshly ground black pepper

TO SERVE
Crusty bread

1 Pour the tomato sauce into a large cast-iron dish or roasting tin and scatter over the feta, spring onions and herbs. Place the dish on the rack and cook for about 5 minutes until the cheese begins to melt.

2 Remove the dish from the rack and add the prawns. Spoon over the ouzo, brandy or wine and baste the prawns with the tomato sauce.

3 Season with plenty of freshly ground black pepper and return the dish to the rack. Cook for about 10 minutes or until the prawns turn pink. Serve with crusty bread to mop up the delicious cooking juices.

tip

If you have a glut of homegrown tomatoes during late summer and autumn you can use any surplus to make your own sauce. Skin and deseed the tomatoes and puree the chopped flesh with a little vegetable stock or tomato juice. For the rest of the year buy a ready-made napolitana pasta sauce or tomato passata (crushed, sieved tomatoes), as out-of-season tomatoes won't have enough flavour.

Spiced tuna with grilled vegetables and warm mustard vinaigrette

The cooking time for the tuna will depend on the thickness of your steaks and how rare your diners like their fish.

PREPARATION TIME: 10 MINUTES + MARINATING

COOKING TIME: LESS THAN 10 MINUTES

SERVES 4

4 x 175g (6oz) tuna steaks
1 tsp paprika
1 tsp ground cumin
1 tsp ground ginger
2 courgettes, sliced lengthways
12 asparagus spears
1 red pepper, deseeded and quartered
1 yellow pepper, deseeded and quartered
6 Tbsp oil

MUSTARD VINAIGRETTE
8 Tbsp olive oil
2 Tbsp cider vinegar
Juice of ½ lemon
1 Tbsp Dijon mustard
Salt and pepper

1 Place the tuna steaks in a shallow dish in a single layer. Mix together the paprika, cumin and ginger and rub over the fish. Leave in a cool place for 1 hour.

2 Brush the tuna steaks and vegetables with the oil and grill them on the rack, in batches if necessary, turning everything over half way. The vegetables will take 3–5 minutes in total, depending on their thickness. For rare tuna allow about 1 minute each side, 3–4 minutes each side for more well done steaks.

3 To make the vinaigrette, whisk all the ingredients together until smooth then warm through in a small pan on the rack. Serve the tuna with the vegetables and the warm vinaigrette spooned over.

Steamed monkfish and prawns in banana leaves

Other white fish fillets could be used for this dish but 'dry' fish such as sole, plaice or sea bass will work better than cod or haddock, both of which produce a lot of liquid that will leak out of the parcels as they cook.

PREPARATION TIME: 15 MINUTES + MARINATING

COOKING TIME: 15 MINUTES

SERVES 4

MARINADE
4 Tbsp coarsely chopped fresh coriander
2 Tbsp coarsely chopped fresh mint
1 lemon grass stalk, finely sliced, or 1 tsp lemon grass purée
2cm (³⁄₄in) piece root ginger, peeled and roughly chopped
4 plump garlic cloves, peeled and roughly chopped
Pinch saffron threads, soaked in 2 Tbsp warm water for 10 minutes
50g (2oz) creamed coconut, grated or roughly chopped
Juice of 2 limes
1 red chilli, deseeded and chopped
2 Tbsp oil
½ tsp salt

FISH
4 x 125g (4¹⁄₂oz) monkfish fillets, skinned
8 large raw prawns, peeled
4 squares banana leaf, approx 25cm (10in)

TO SERVE
Rice
Green salad

1 Put all the marinade ingredients in a blender or food processor and reduce to a paste. If you don't have a blender, chop everything as finely as possible by hand and mix with the saffron and its soaking water, lime juice and oil.

2 Lay the monkfish fillets and prawns in a single layer in a shallow dish and spread with the paste. Set aside to marinate for 30 minutes.

3 Wrap a monkfish fillet and two prawns in each banana leaf and secure the parcels with cocktail sticks. The parcels must be well secured so the juices don't leak out during cooking.

4 Place the parcels in a steamer and cook on top of the chiminea for 15 minutes. Open up the parcels on serving plates and serve with rice and a green salad.

tip

Packs of banana leaves pre-cut into large squares are available from Oriental supermarkets but if there isn't one near you, squares of baking parchment would work perfectly well. Use two squares of parchment to enclose the food – top and bottom – and fold the edges over neatly to make a tight seal. Dip banana leaves in hot water for a few seconds before using to soften them and make them easier to handle.

King prawns with chermoula

Chermoula is a spicy Moroccan paste of garlic, spices, lemon and herbs that makes a good seasoning mix for seafood or chicken. Use raw king prawns and butterfly them before marinating so they absorb all the chermoula's flavours.

PREPARATION TIME: 15 MINUTES + MARINATING

COOKING TIME: 3–4 MINUTES

SERVES 4

2 fat garlic cloves, peeled and crushed
1 tsp ground coriander
1 tsp harissa paste
2 Tbsp chopped fresh coriander
Finely grated rind and juice of 2 lemons
3 Tbsp olive oil
16 raw king prawns, shell on

1 In a bowl, mix together the garlic, ground coriander, harissa, chopped coriander, lemon rind and juice and olive oil.

2 Remove the heads from the prawns but leave the shells and tails on. Using a small sharp knife, cut down the back of each one, about half way through the flesh, and pull out the black thread running down it.

3 Turn the prawns over and press gently to flatten and open them out. Add the prawns to the bowl, turning them so they are coated in the marinade and leave for 30 minutes.

4 Cook the prawns on the grill rack for about 3–4 minutes, shell side down, or until the prawns turn pink and opaque. Serve at once.

tip

The marinade could also be used with chicken and white fish, either as joints or whole fish or cubed and threaded on to skewers for kebabs.

4 main courses – meat

Mexican steaks
Honey and mustard gammon
Cranberry and rosemary-glazed lamb steaks
Butterflied leg of lamb
Slow-braised beef with brown ale
Sunset strip steak with California salad
Minted lamb and redcurrant cutlets
Souvlakia
Lamb koftas
Kleftiko
Jamaican jerk pork steaks
Fragrant Asian lamb cutlets
Peppered beef and glass noodle salad
Herb and spice-rubbed steaks
Gingered pork chops

Mexican steaks

The steaks can be served with either a cool, spicy salsa or creamy mayonnaise, according to personal taste. New potatoes, crusty bread and green salad all make good accompaniments to this recipe.

PREPARATION TIME: 10 MINUTES + MARINATING

COOKING TIME: LESS THAN 5 MINUTES

SERVES: 4

4 sirloin or rump steaks, fat trimmed off
1 tsp dried chilli flakes
½ tsp ground allspice
1 tsp smoked paprika
1 tsp fresh garlic purée
4 Tbsp red wine
Olive oil for brushing

TO SERVE
Mango, red onion and cucumber salsa (see page 162)
  or Dill and horseradish mayonnaise (see page 150)
Green salad

1 Place the steaks side by side in a shallow dish. Mix together the chilli flakes, allspice, paprika, garlic and red wine and pour over the steaks, turning them over so they are coated in the marinade. Leave to marinate for 3–4 hours or overnight.

2 Lift the steaks from the dish and brush with olive oil. Cook on the grill rack for 2 minutes on each side, or longer depending on how well done you like your meat.

3 Leave to rest for 5 minutes in a warm place before serving with the salsa and salad.

 tip

An alternative way to serve the steaks is to cut them into thin slices across the grain of the meat once cooked and to pile the slices into pitta pockets or tortilla wraps with a mix of salad ingredients and relishes.

Honey and mustard gammon

The lightly scorched peach halves used in this recipe make a more unusual accompaniment to the gammon than traditional pineapple.

PREPARATION TIME: 10 MINUTES + MARINATING

COOKING TIME: 5–7 MINUTES

SERVES 4

4 gammon steaks
4 Tbsp sunflower oil
1 tsp wholegrain mustard
2 Tbsp red wine vinegar
1 tsp clear honey
4 ripe but firm peaches, halved and stoned
40g (1½oz) butter, melted
2 Tbsp caster sugar

TO SERVE
New potatoes
Green salad

1 Snip the edges of the gammon at 2.5 cm (1 in) intervals with a pair of kitchen scissors so the steaks don't curl on the rack as they cook. If the steaks still have their rind left on, cut this off first.

2 Place the gammon steaks in a shallow dish. Whisk together the oil, mustard, vinegar and honey and pour over the gammon, turning the steaks until they are coated. Leave to marinate for 3–4 hours.

2 Lift the gammon from the dish and grill on the rack for 5–7 minutes, depending on the thickness of the steaks. Turn them over once or twice and brush with any marinade left in the dish.

3 Brush the cut sides of the peaches with melted butter and dust with caster sugar. Once the gammon is cooked, place the peach halves, cut side down, on the rack for about 30 seconds so the flesh scorches and browns slightly.

4 Serve the gammon with the peaches. Accompany with new potatoes and a green salad.

Cranberry and rosemary-glazed lamb steaks

Lamb-leg steaks are much meatier than smaller cuts such as chump or best-end chops. You could use chops but allow 2–3 per person.

PREPARATION TIME: 10 MINUTES + MARINATING

COOKING TIME: 10–15 MINUTES

SERVES 4

4 lamb steaks, cut from the leg
2 Tbsp cranberry jelly
1 Tbsp balsamic vinegar
2 tsp Dijon mustard
1 Tbsp chopped fresh rosemary leaves
2 Tbsp olive oil

1 Place the lamb steaks in a single layer in a shallow dish. In a small bowl, beat the cranberry jelly until smooth, then mix in the vinegar, mustard, rosemary and oil.

2 Spoon the mixture over the lamb, turning the steaks over until well coated. Leave to marinate for 3–4 hours or overnight.

3 Grill the steaks on the rack for 10–15 minutes, depending on how thick they are and how well-cooked you like your meat. Turn them over once and baste or brush with any marinade left in the dish.

tip

Before mixing the other ingredients with the cranberry jelly, beat it well first to loosen its texture so it becomes smooth and runny. Other jellies could be used instead of cranberry such as mint, redcurrant, quince or orange jelly marmalade. Strip the needle-like rosemary leaves off their stalks and chop them finely before adding to the marinade.

Butterflied leg of lamb

Boning the lamb is much easier than it sounds but if you're nervous of tackling it yourself, ask the butcher to do it for you – order it in advance if you shop when he's likely to be busy!

PREPARATION TIME: 25 MINUTES + MARINATING AND RESTING

COOKING TIME: 40 MINUTES

SERVES 6–8

2.25kg (5lb) leg of lamb
Leaves from 6 sprigs thyme
Leaves from 6 sprigs rosemary, finely chopped
4 garlic cloves, peeled and crushed
1 Tbsp clear honey
Finely grated rind and juice of 1 lemon
4 Tbsp olive oil
Freshly ground black pepper

1 To butterfly the lamb, find where the long bone runs down the length of the leg quite close to the surface and cut open the meat by working a sharp knife down one side of the bone. Continue cutting around the bone, carefully peeling the meat back on either side until you can take out the bone.

2 Cut the meat away from the small group of bones at the thicker end of the joint until the leg is opened up and you can lift them out. The boned meat will be shaped like a butterfly, hence its name.

3 Mix together the thyme, rosemary, garlic, honey, lemon rind, juice, oil and pepper. Lay the lamb in a shallow dish, pour over the herb and garlic mixture and leave to marinate for 24 hours.

4 Roast the lamb on the grill rack for about 40 minutes for medium rare, or longer if you prefer your meat well done, turning over once or twice.

5 Transfer the lamb to a board and cover with foil. Leave to rest for 5 minutes before carving.

tip

The lamb needs plenty of time to marinate to let it absorb all the garlicky herb flavours, so prepare it the day before you plan to cook it.

Slow-braised beef with brown ale

This dish needs to be left for several hours to simmer gently on top of the chiminea so that the beef becomes beautifully tender in the rich gravy. Instead of brown ale you could use Guinness, or red wine to turn it into a bourguignon.

PREPARATION TIME: 20 MINUTES

COOKING TIME: APPROX. 2½–3 HOURS

SERVES 4

3 Tbsp oil
700g (1lb 9oz) lean braising steak, cut into 2.5cm (1in) cubes
25g (1oz) plain flour
300ml (10fl oz) beef stock
Approx. 330ml (11fl oz) brown ale (1 bottle or can, depending on size)
1 x 230g (8oz) tin chopped tomatoes
1 tsp Worcestershire sauce
1 tsp black treacle or molasses
Salt and pepper
2 large onions, peeled and chopped
225g (8oz) large carrots, sliced
225g (8oz) button mushrooms
8 medium potatoes, peeled and cut into chunks

1 Heat the oil in a flameproof casserole on a conventional hob and seal the steak in batches, removing the pieces from the casserole as they brown.

2 Mix the flour with half the stock and add to the casserole with the remaining stock, the brown ale, tomatoes, Worcestershire sauce, treacle and seasoning. Bring to the boil, stirring until the sauce is smooth and thickened, and simmer for 1 minute.

3 Add the onions, carrots and mushrooms and return the beef to the casserole. Cover tightly with foil and a lid and cook on top of the chiminea for 1¹/2 hours.

4 Add the potatoes and cook for a further 1–1¹/2 hours or until the beef and vegetables are tender. Check the casserole from time to time to make sure the cooking liquid does not evaporate too much, especially if the lid is not a very tight fit. Top up with more stock or water if needed.

Sunset strip steak with California salad

Californians are famous for their low-fat, healthy-eating regimes so dieters or anyone watching their weight can enjoy this dish without feeling they've over-indulged. Instead of thick, ready-cut steaks, buy the meat in one piece and cut it into thin steaks yourself or ask the butcher to do it for you.

PREPARATION TIME: 15 MINUTES + MARINATING

COOKING TIME: ABOUT 5 MINUTES

SERVES 4

600g (1lb 5oz) rump or sirloin steak
1 Tbsp ground coriander
1 tsp paprika
3 Tbsp olive oil
1 Tbsp balsamic vinegar

SALAD
225g (8oz) French beans, blanched for 2 minutes
1 red pepper, deseeded and thinly sliced
1 large seedless orange, peeled and segmented
2 celery sticks, cut into matchsticks
1 kiwi fruit, peeled and sliced
75g (3oz) black olives
3 Tbsp vinaigrette dressing, full-fat or low-fat, as you prefer

1 Cut the steak into eight pieces across the grain of the meat and place them in a bowl or shallow dish. Mix together the coriander, paprika, olive oil and vinegar and pour over the steak, turning the pieces until coated. Leave to marinate for 3–4 hours or longer.

2 For the salad, mix the beans, red pepper, orange, celery, kiwi fruit and olives in a bowl and toss with the dressing.

3 Lift the steak from the marinade and grill on the rack for 2 minutes on each side or until done to your liking, basting or brushing with any marinade left in the bowl. Serve the steak with the salad.

Minted lamb and redcurrant cutlets

Mint and redcurrant jelly are natural partners for lamb and this marinade is given an extra tang with the addition of paprika and red wine vinegar. The same mix could be used for marinating lamb steaks and kebabs.

PREPARATION TIME: 10 MINUTES + MARINATING

COOKING TIME: 10 MINUTES

SERVES 4

8 large or 12 small lamb cutlets
2 Tbsp redcurrant jelly
1 tsp paprika
2 Tbsp chopped fresh mint
1 Tbsp red wine vinegar
2 Tbsp olive oil

TO SERVE
Mixed bean bowl (see page 137)

1 Place the lamb cutlets in a single layer in a shallow dish. In a small bowl, beat the redcurrant jelly until smooth, then beat in the paprika, mint, wine vinegar and olive oil.

2 Spread the mixture over the cutlets, turning them over so they are well coated, and leave to marinate for 3–4 hours or until ready to cook.

3 Grill the cutlets on the rack for 5 minutes. Turn them over, brush with any marinade left in the dish and grill for a further 4–5 minutes or until done to your liking.

4 Serve with the mixed bean bowl.

 ## tip

If the tips of the cutlet bones are exposed, cover them with small pieces of foil so they don't blacken and burn on the grill.

Souvlakia

The name for these kebabs comes from the Greek word 'souvla', meaning a skewer or spit, and they can be made using cubes of either lean pork or lamb. Pork will need to be cooked for slightly longer as it must be done all the way through but the lamb can be as rare or as well done as you prefer.

PREPARATION TIME: 15 MINUTES + PLUS MARINATING

COOKING TIME: LESS THAN 10 MINUTES

SERVES 6

1kg (2lb 4oz) lean boneless leg of lamb or pork, cut into 2cm
   (³/₄in) cubes
1 Tbsp ground coriander
2 tsp dried oregano
2 tsp dried thyme
2 bay leaves
175ml (6fl oz) extra virgin olive oil
3 Tbsp red wine vinegar
Freshly ground black pepper

TO SERVE
Lemon wedges
Tzatziki (see page 158)

1 Place the meat cubes in a bowl. Mix together the coriander, herbs, bay leaves, oil, vinegar and pepper.

2 Pour the marinade over the meat and leave to marinate for 3–4 hours, or until ready to cook.

3 Thread the meat on to skewers and cook on the grill rack or a hot plate placed on the rack for 5–8 minutes, turning over regularly until the meat is crusty and brown and cooked to your liking.

4 Serve with lemon wedges to squeeze over and Tzatziki.

tip

Turn the kebabs over regularly during cooking so the meat browns evenly on all sides. If your chiminea has a spit roaster, the meat could be cut into larger chunks and cooked on that.

Lamb koftas

To prevent the meat breaking up, press it firmly around the skewers and chill the kebabs before cooking.

PREPARATION TIME: 20 MINUTES + PLUS MARINATING

COOKING TIME: 15 MINUTES

SERVES 4

500g (1lb 2oz) lean lamb mince
2 garlic cloves, peeled and crushed
2 tsp ground coriander
1 tsp ground cumin
1 tsp paprika
2 Tbsp tomato purée
75g (3oz) ground almonds
2 Tbsp finely chopped fresh coriander
Freshly ground black pepper
1 egg, beaten
Oil for brushing

TO SERVE
Naan bread
Salad
Mango chutney

1 Put the mince in a bowl and break up with a fork. Add the garlic, spices, tomato purée, ground almonds and coriander and stir until evenly mixed.

2 Season with pepper and stir in the beaten egg to bind the mixture together.

3 With damp hands, divide the mixture into 12 equal portions and press each around a short skewer in a sausage shape. Chill for 3–4 hours or until ready to cook.

4 Heat a hot plate or griddle pan on the grill rack, place the koftas on top and cook for about 15 minutes, turning them over regularly until well browned.

5 Serve with naan bread, salad and mango chutney.

Kleftiko

A classic Greek dish where a leg of lamb is seasoned with garlic, herbs, lemon juice and olive oil and then slowly roasted in a tightly sealed container so none of the delicious juices and aromas are lost. The origins of the dish are many and varied, one belief being that when villages were threatened by outlaws, the men would set out to fight them off and when they returned, the slowly roasted lamb would be cooked to perfection.

PREPARATION TIME: 15 MINUTES

COOKING TIME: 2¼ HOURS

SERVES 6

1.5kg (3 ¼ lb) leg of lamb, bone in
3 garlic cloves, peeled and cut into slivers
Freshly ground black pepper
1 onion, peeled and sliced
1 carrot, peeled and sliced
2 celery sticks, chopped
2 bay leaves
4 sprigs thyme
4 sprigs rosemary
300ml (10fl oz) red wine
4 Tbsp olive oil
1 x 400g (14oz) tin chopped tomatoes

1 Cut small slits all over the lamb with the point of a sharp knife and push the garlic into the slits. Season the lamb with plenty of freshly ground black pepper and place in a deep roasting tin.

2 Add the onion, carrot, celery and herbs to the tin, pour in the wine and olive oil and spoon the tomatoes around the lamb.

3 Cover the tin with foil, tucking it under the edges of the tin to make a tight seal. Cook on the grill rack for 2 hours, topping up the coals as necessary. Remove the foil and cook for a further 15 minutes so the top of the lamb browns and begins to crisp.

4 Serve the lamb cut into thick slices with the vegetables and cooking juices.

Jamaican jerk pork steaks

There must be as many different jerk blends in Jamaica as there are cooks. Most are simply a mix of dried herbs and spices but others are given an extra kick with a generous tot of the local rum stirred in for good measure.

PREPARATION TIME: 10 MINUTES + MARINATING TIME

COOKING TIME: 10–15 MINUTES

SERVES 4

600g (1lb 5oz) pork loin steaks
1 tsp fresh garlic purée
1 tsp fresh ginger purée
1/4 tsp ground allspice
1 Tbsp hot chilli sauce, or to taste
1 Tbsp brown sugar
2 Tbsp oil

TO SERVE
Jacket potatoes (see page 141)
or Roasted sweet potato wedges (see page 139)
Mango, red onion and cucumber salsa (see page 162)

1 Trim any fat from the pork steaks and place them in a single layer in a dish.

2 Mix together the garlic purée, ginger purée and allspice. Stir in the chilli sauce, brown sugar and oil and spread over the pork. Marinate in a cool place for several hours, turning the pork over once or twice.

3 Lift the steaks from the dish, allowing any excess marinade to drip back into the dish, and grill on the rack for about 10–15 minutes, turning the pork over once or twice and brushing with any remaining marinade, until cooked through.

4 Serve with jacket or wedge potatoes, and mango, red onion and cucumber salsa.

tip

Chicken joints can be used instead of pork but the cooking time will need to be adjusted according to the thickness of the meat.

Fragrant Asian lamb cutlets

If you use garlic and ginger in a lot of your marinades – as in this recipe – it's worth making your own purée. Coarsely crush, grate or chop equal amounts of peeled garlic cloves and fresh root ginger and blend together in a small food processor with a little vegetable until smooth. Store the purée in a screw top jar in the fridge and use as required.

PREPARATION TIME: 10 MINUTES + MARINATING

COOKING TIME: 8–10 MINUTES

SERVES 4

1 Tbsp chilli purée
4 Tbsp dark soy sauce
1 tsp fresh garlic purée
1 tsp fresh ginger purée
2 tsp sesame oil
3 Tbsp mirin
3 Tbsp rice vinegar or white wine vinegar
12 lamb cutlets

1 Whisk together the chilli purée, soy sauce, garlic purée and ginger purée, sesame oil, mirin and vinegar with a fork until combined.

2 Place the lamb cutlets in a single layer in a shallow dish and spread with the marinade. Leave to marinate for several hours or overnight, turning the cutlets over once so they absorb the flavours evenly.

3 Grill the cutlets on the rack for 8–10 minutes or until done to your liking, basting or brushing with any juices left in the dish while cooking.

tip

Mirin is a sweet rice wine widely used in Japanese cooking, particularly for sauces and marinades. Most large supermarkets stock it amongst their Oriental ingredients but if you have difficulty finding it, use 1 Tbsp sugar instead, stirring the sugar into the soy sauce first so it dissolves. The recipe uses ordinary sesame oil but if only the toasted variety is available, reduce the quantity to a few drops as toasted sesame oil is very strong and it will overpower other flavours.

Peppered beef and glass noodle salad

Also known as transparent or cellophane noodles, glass noodles are made from dried mung beans and are most commonly used in Oriental soups.

PREPARATION TIME: 20 MINUTES + STANDING

COOKING TIME: LESS THAN 15 MINUTES

SERVES 4

400g (14oz) fillet steak, in one piece
2 Tbsp oil
2 Tbsp green or black peppercorns, crushed or coarsely ground
115g (4oz) glass noodles, soaked according to the packet instructions
2 Tbsp Thai fish sauce (nam pla)
2 garlic cloves, peeled and crushed
Juice of 2 limes or 1 lemon
1 tsp sugar
2 Tbsp chopped fresh mint
100g (3½oz) rocket or mixed salad leaves
6 cherry tomatoes, halved
½ cucumber, sliced
4 spring onions, shredded, to garnish

1 Brush the steak with the oil and roll in the crushed peppercorns. Cook on the grill rack for 2–3 minutes on each side until well browned all over for rare, or longer if you prefer it medium or well done. Remove from the heat and set aside for 10 minutes.

2 Drain the soaked noodles, pat dry with kitchen paper and place in a bowl. Mix together the fish sauce, crushed garlic, lime or lemon juice, sugar and mint, stirring until the sugar dissolves. Pour the dressing over the noodles, stirring until they are well coated.

3 Divide the rocket or salad leaves, tomato halves and cucumber slices between four serving plates and pile the noodles on top.

4 Carve the beef into slices as thinly as possible and arrange over the noodles. Garnish with the shredded spring onions and spoon over any dressing left in the noodle bowl.

Herb and spice-rubbed steaks

The best cuts of steak for grilling are rump, sirloin, rib-eye and fillet as they're the most tender.

PREPARATION TIME: 10 MINUTES + MARINATING

COOKING TIME: LESS THAN 5 MINUTES

SERVES: 4

1 tsp ground black pepper
½ tsp mustard powder
2 tsp dried herbes de Provence
4 sirloin or rump steaks about 3cm (1¼in) thick
Extra virgin olive oil for brushing

TO SERVE
Jacket potatoes (see page 141)
Coleslaw (see page 140)

1 Mix together the pepper, mustard and herbes de Provence and rub the mixture over both sides of the steaks. Place on a plate or board and leave to marinate for 3–4 hours or longer.

2 Brush the steaks with olive oil and cook on the grill rack for 2 minutes on each side for medium rare or longer if you prefer your meat well done.

3 Serve with jacket potatoes and coleslaw.

tip

Trim excess fat from the meat before cooking so it doesn't drip down on to the coals and catch fire and leave the steaks to stand for a few minutes before serving so the juices have time to run back through the meat.

Gingered pork chops

Valentine pork steaks are ideal for this recipe (thick slices of pork loin cut through the middle and opened out to make a heart-shaped steak). Most good butchers and larger supermarket meat counters should sell them or be able to prepare them for you but, if not, use boneless loin chops.

PREPARATION TIME: 10 MINUTES + PLUS MARINATING

COOKING TIME: 10 MINUTES

SERVES 4

4 boneless pork chops or pork steaks
1 tsp fresh ginger purée
4 Tbsp teriyaki marinade (bottled or use the marinade recipe
   for teriyaki salmon on page 53)
1 tsp brown sugar
2 garlic cloves, peeled and crushed

TO SERVE
Jacket potatoes (see page 141)
Pepper, tomato and sweetcorn relish (see page 151)

1 Place the pork in a single layer in a shallow dish. Mix together the ginger, teriyaki marinade, brown sugar and garlic, stirring until the sugar dissolves.

2 Pour the mixture over the pork and leave to marinate for 3–4 hours or overnight.

3 Grill the pork for 10 minutes on the rack or until cooked through, turning the meat over occasionally and basting or brushing with any marinade left in the dish.

4 Serve with jacket potatoes and relish.

5 main courses
– poultry

Chicken, pomegranate and nectarine salad
Roast chicken with lemon and garlic
Coconut, coriander and lemon chicken
Marmalade and soy-glazed duck with mango
  salad
Chicken, chorizo and mozzarella baps
Honey chilli chicken
Chinese duck with pancakes
Caribbean chicken
Tandoori chicken
Chicken piri piri
Poussins roasted with Mediterranean herbs
Thai chicken bites
Yakitori chicken sticks
Chicken, olive and saffron tagine
Five-spice chicken

Chicken, pomegranate and nectarine salad

Pomegranates are one of our new superfoods so adding the seeds to this salad makes it extra healthy. To remove the seeds from a pomegranate, cut the fruit in half and dig them out with a skewer or the point of a sharp knife. Alternatively, tap the back of the fruit firmly with a spoon and the seeds should just fall out. Whichever method you choose, hold the pomegranate over a bowl to catch the seeds and any drops of the beautiful pink juice, which can be added to the dressing.

PREPARATION TIME: 15 MINUTES + MARINATING

COOKING TIME: 15 MINUTES

SERVES: 4

4 boneless chicken breasts, skinned
6 Tbsp olive oil
1 Tbsp chopped fresh mint
1 Tbsp lemon juice
1 tsp Dijon mustard
2 Tbsp red wine vinegar
Freshly ground black pepper
50g (2oz) wild rocket
4 large lettuce leaves, e.g. batavia, Cos or iceberg, shredded
2 ripe nectarines, stoned and cut into wedges
Seeds of 1 pomegranate

1 Put the chicken breasts in a single layer in a dish. Whisk together 2 Tbsp olive oil, the mint, lemon juice and mustard and spoon over the chicken, turning the breasts over until they are coated. Leave to marinate for 3–4 hours.

2 Remove the chicken from the marinade and cook on the grill rack for about 15 minutes or until done, turning over once or twice and brushing with any marinade left in the dish.

3 While the chicken is cooking, whisk together the remaining olive oil, red wine vinegar and black pepper to make the dressing. Divide the rocket, lettuce and nectarines between four serving plates.

4 Carve the cooked chicken into thick slices and arrange on top of the salad. Drizzle over the oil and vinegar dressing and scatter with the pomegranate seeds.

Roast chicken with lemon and garlic

It's important to keep the charcoal topped up so the temperature remains constant for the whole of the cooking time in this recipe. If you have a spit-roaster attachment for your chiminea, this would be an ideal recipe for using it.

PREPARATION TIME: 15 MINUTES

COOKING TIME: $1^{1}/_{4}$–$1^{1}/_{2}$ HOURS

SERVES 4

1.4kg (3lb) chicken
Freshly ground black pepper
2 Tbsp chopped fresh parsley
1 Tbsp chopped fresh oregano or marjoram
1 Tbsp pesto
1 lemon, halved
4 large garlic cloves, unpeeled
4 Tbsp extra virgin olive oil

1 Rinse the chicken inside and out and pat dry with kitchen paper. Season the cavity with freshly ground black pepper. Mix together the parsley, oregano or marjoram and pesto.

2 Pull up the skin at the top of the breast bone, taking care not to split it, and, with the fingers of your other hand, gently separate the skin from the breast working from the neck end, Spread the pesto mixture over the breast meat, fold the skin back over it and secure in place with a cocktail stick.

3 Put the lemon halves and garlic cloves in the body cavity and tie the legs together with fine string. Lift the chicken into a roasting tin and brush all over with the olive oil.

4 Cover the tin with foil and cook on the grill rack for $1^{1}/_{4}$–$1^{1}/_{2}$ hours, opening the foil for the last 20 minutes or so to brown the skin. Check for doneness by piercing the thickest part of the drumstick with a skewer and the juices should run clear. Alternatively, test with a meat probe.

5 Cover with foil again and leave to stand for 10 minutes before carving.

Coconut, coriander and lemon chicken

The coriander and lemon give the chicken a spicy tang, whilst the coconut milk helps to keep the flesh moist and tender. New potato salad with bacon, rocket and spring onions makes the perfect accompaniment to this quick and easy chicken dish.

PREPARATION TIME: 10 MINUTES + MARINATING

COOKING TIME: 15 MINUTES

SERVES 4

4 boneless chicken breasts, skinned
2 tsp ground coriander
2 Tbsp sunflower oil
150ml (5fl oz) coconut milk
Freshly ground black pepper
2 limes, halved

TO SERVE
New potato salad with bacon, rocket and spring onions
  (see page 143)

1 Cut several slashes into the thickest part of the flesh of each chicken breast and place them side by side in a shallow dish.

2 Whisk together the coriander, oil, coconut milk and black pepper and pour over the chicken, turning the breasts over until coated. Leave to marinate for 3–4 hours.

3 Lift the chicken breasts from the marinade and cook on the grill rack for about 15 minutes or until cooked through, turning the breasts over once or twice and brushing with any marinade left in the dish.

4 Remove the chicken from the rack, squeeze over the juice from the limes and serve.

tip

If you use canned coconut milk it can sometimes separate
in the tin so give the tin a good shake before you open it.

Marmalade and soy-glazed duck with mango salad

The marmalade and soy sauce caramelize to a delicious sticky coating on the duck in this colourful dish.

PREPARATION TIME: 15 MINUTES + STANDING

COOKING TIME: 15 MINUTES

SERVES 4

4 duck breasts
2 Tbsp orange jelly marmalade (or any marmalade with large
   pieces of peel removed)
2 Tbsp dark soy sauce
1 Tbsp fresh ginger purée

SALAD
6 Tbsp sunflower oil
2 Tbsp rice vinegar
Freshly ground black pepper
50g (2oz) rocket
1 bunch watercress, coarse stalks removed
1 large ripe mango, peeled and chopped
1 red pepper, deseeded and finely chopped
1 red onion, peeled and finely sliced
1 avocado, peeled, deseeded and chopped

1 Heat a griddle on the grill rack, add the duck breasts skin side down and cook for 10 minutes, turning the breasts over once or twice.

2 Beat the marmalade until smooth and mix in the soy sauce and ginger. Pour off any excess fat from the griddle and spread the marmalade mixture over the duck skins. Cook them for a further 5 minutes, skin side down, until caramelized. Remove the duck from the pan and place on a plate or board, cover with foil and set aside for 5 minutes before carving into thin slices.

3 To make the dressing, whisk together the oil and vinegar with plenty of freshly ground black pepper. Put the rocket and watercress in a bowl and add the mango, red pepper, red onion and avocado. Arrange the duck slices on top, pour over the dressing and serve at once.

Chicken, chorizo and mozzarella baps

The drier cooking mozzarella works better in this recipe as soft mozzarella balls packed in water contain too much moisture that will make the baps soggy.

PREPARATION TIME: 15 MINUTES + MARINATING

COOKING TIME: LESS THAN 20 MINUTES

SERVES 4

2 boneless chicken breasts, skinned
2 tsp paprika
1 tsp sugar
2 Tbsp orange juice
2 Tbsp oil
175g (6oz) chorizo sausage, cut into long 5mm (¼in) slices
4 large baps
1 Tbsp red pesto
2 tomatoes, sliced
4 slices cooking mozzarella cheese

1 Put the chicken breasts in a shallow dish. Mix together the paprika, sugar, orange juice and oil and spoon over the chicken, turning the breasts over until coated. Leave to marinate for 3–4 hours or longer.

2 Lift the chicken from the marinade and grill on the rack for about 15 minutes or until cooked through, turning over occasionally and basting or brushing with any marinade left in the dish.

3 When the chicken is almost ready, grill the chorizo slices on the rack for 1 minute on each side so they crisp a little on the outside, and lightly toast the cut sides of the baps. Cut the chicken into thin slices.

4 Spread the bottom half of the baps with the pesto and stand them on a small baking sheet or roasting tray. Top with the chicken, chorizo and tomato slices and lay a mozzarella slice on top of each.

5 Put the baking sheet on the rack for 1–2 minutes until the cheese starts to melt. Remove, add the bap lids and serve.

Honey chilli chicken

You can remove the skin from the chicken or leave it on as you prefer in this recipe. If you leave it on, cut several slashes in the meat with a sharp knife so the flavours of the glaze can penetrate right into the flesh.

PREPARATION TIME: 10 MINUTES

COOKING TIME: 25 MINUTES

SERVES 4

8 chicken thighs, skin on
2 Tbsp olive oil
2 tsp dried thyme
2 Tbsp clear honey
1 tsp sweet chilli sauce
Freshly ground black pepper

TO SERVE
Mixed salad
Coleslaw (see page 140)
Pepper, tomato and sweetcorn relish (see page 160)

1 Place the chicken thighs in a single layer in shallow roasting tin.

2 Mix together the olive oil, thyme, honey, chilli sauce and black pepper and spoon over the chicken.

3 Grill the chicken on the rack for about 10 minutes. Grill for a further 15 minutes basting the chicken with the honey mixture from time to time until the thighs are cooked through, golden brown and sticky.

tip

Chicken breasts could be used instead of thighs or even chicken wings, but snip off the wing tips with kitchen scissors before cooking.

Chinese duck with pancakes

Chinese-style pancakes can be bought from Oriental stores and some larger supermarkets also sell them.

PREPARATION TIME: 15 MINUTES + STANDING

COOKING TIME: 15 MINUTES

SERVES 4

4 duck breasts
2 Tbsp oyster sauce
1 Tbsp golden syrup
1 Tbsp rice vinegar or white wine vinegar
1 tsp Chinese five-spice powder
1 tsp fresh ginger purée

TO SERVE
16–20 Chinese-style pancakes, warmed
1 small bottle Chinese plum sauce or hoi sin sauce
½ cucumber, cut into matchsticks
8 spring onions, shredded

1 Heat a ridged grill pan or cast-iron griddle on the grill rack and lay the duck breasts on it skin side down. Cook for 10 minutes, turning over once or twice until evenly browned. Pour off any excess fat.

2 Mix together the oyster sauce, golden syrup, vinegar, five-spice powder and ginger purée and spread over the duck skin. Continue to cook for about 5 minutes until the skin caramelizes and crisps. Meanwhile, warm the pancakes in a foil parcel placed on top of the chiminea while the duck is below.

3 Remove the duck and place on a board, cover with a sheet of foil to keep it warm and leave to stand for 5 minutes before slicing the breasts as thinly as possible.

4 To serve, spread the pancakes with a little plum or hoi sin sauce, add duck slices, cucumber and spring onions and roll up to eat.

Caribbean chicken

Coconut cream is richer than ordinary coconut milk and can be bought in small Tetra Paks from supermarkets, but use coconut milk if you prefer.

PREPARATION TIME: 15 MINUTES + MARINATING

COOKING TIME: 15–20 MINUTES

SERVES 4

4 boneless chicken breasts, skin on
1 x 200ml (7fl oz) carton coconut cream
Juice of 1 lime
$1/2$ tsp ground allspice
3 Tbsp soft brown sugar
2 mangoes
4 pineapple slices

TO SERVE
Calypso rice salad (see page 147)
Curried mayonnaise (see page 150)

1 Slash the chicken breasts several times with a sharp knife and place them side by side in a shallow dish. Mix together the coconut cream, lime juice, allspice and 1 Tbsp of the sugar and pour over the chicken, turning the breasts over so they are well coated. Leave to marinate for 3–4 hours.

2 Lift the chicken from the dish and grill on the rack for about 15 minutes or until cooked through, turning the breasts over once or twice and brushing with any remaining marinade.

3 When the chicken is almost ready, cut two thick slices from each mango, cutting down each side as close to the fibrous central stone as you can. Sprinkle the remaining 2 Tbsp sugar over the mango and pineapple slices and grill for 1–2 minutes on the rack until lightly caramelized.

4 Serve the chicken and fruit hot with Calypso rice salad and Curried mayonnaise.

 ## tip

The best way to tell if fruit (particularly tropical fruit) is ripe is to smell it. If a mango or pineapple has no sweet aroma, it's unlikely to have much taste either.

Tandoori chicken

Made of clay and heated with charcoal or wood, an Indian tandoor is first cousin to a Mexican chiminea, and both ovens are equally good for cooking this classic Indian dish. If you want to mimic the vibrant red of some tandoori chicken served in this country, you'll need to add food colouring to the marinating mix.

PREPARATION TIME: 10 MINUTES + MARINATING

COOKING TIME: 10 MINUTES

SERVES 4

8 chicken thighs or 4 boneless chicken breasts, skinned
2 Tbsp tandoori curry paste
200g (7oz) natural yogurt
Juice of 1 lemon
2 Tbsp oil
¼ cucumber, finely chopped
2 Tbsp chopped fresh coriander
1 lemon, cut into wedges

TO SERVE
Naan bread
Leafy mixed salad

1 Cut the chicken into 2.5cm (1in) pieces and spread out in a shallow dish.

2 Mix together the curry paste, 4 Tbsp of the yoghurt, the lemon juice and oil and spoon over the chicken, turning the pieces over until coated. Leave to marinate for 3–4 hours.

3 Thread the chicken pieces on to skewers and grill on the rack for 10 minutes, turning over occasionally and brushing with any marinade left in the dish.

4 Stir the cucumber and coriander into the remaining yogurt and serve with the chicken. Accompany with lemon wedges to squeeze over.

tip

If you're feeding a crowd chicken thighs are cheaper and taste just as good as breasts.

Chicken piri piri

Piri piri are tiny, blazingly hot chillies that are very popular in Portugal where they grow. They make a fiery sauce for glazing chicken joints that are then roasted on a barbecue or in a conventional oven. If piri piri are unavailable, but you still want the heat, use small, bird's-eye chillies instead. Alternatively, substitute larger, milder chillies if you prefer.

PREPARATION TIME: 15 MINUTES + MARINATING

COOKING TIME: 15 MINUTES

SERVES 4

4 small red chillies or 2 large red chillies, deseeded, roughly chopped
3 garlic cloves, peeled and roughly chopped
1 tsp salt
1 tsp chopped fresh thyme
1 tsp paprika
5 Tbsp extra virgin olive oil
5 Tbsp red wine vinegar
8 chicken thighs, skin on

TO SERVE
Tomato and cucumber salad

1 To make the piri piri sauce, roughly chop the chillies and place in a blender with the garlic, salt, thyme, paprika, olive oil and vinegar. Process until smooth.

2 Spread half the sauce over the chicken thighs and marinate for 2–3 hours.

3 Grill the chicken on the rack for 15 minutes or until cooked through, turning the thighs over once or twice and brushing with the remaining piri piri sauce.

4 Serve with a cooling tomato and cucumber salad.

 tip

The piri piri mix could also be used with king prawns or full-flavoured fish fillets like tuna or swordfish, but reduce the marinating time to 1 hour.

Poussins roasted with Mediterranean herbs

Poussins have sweet juicy flesh and are delicious grilled over an open fire. Some are sold already spatchcocked (with the backbone removed and pressed flat), but it's easy to do it yourself (steps 1 and 2).

PREPARATION TIME: 25 MINUTES + PLUS MARINATING

COOKING TIME: 35 MINUTES

SERVES 2

2 poussins, each weighing approx. 450g (1lb)
50g (2oz) butter, softened
1 Tbsp Dijon mustard
2 fat garlic cloves, peeled and crushed
1 tsp thyme leaves
1 Tbsp finely chopped rosemary leaves
1 Tbsp chopped fresh oregano
Freshly ground black pepper

TO SERVE
1 lemon, cut into wedges

1 Using poultry shears or heavy kitchen scissors, cut down each side of the backbone of the poussins and remove it. Turn the birds over and open them out, pushing the legs and wings to the sides. Work your fingers under the skin at the neck and carefully pull or cut out the wishbone without tearing the skin.

2 Press down heavily on the breastbone of each poussin until they are quite flat. Push two skewers diagonally through the flesh to hold the birds in shape and cut off the wing tips.

3 Mix together the butter, mustard, garlic, thyme, rosemary and oregano and season with plenty of freshly ground black pepper. Spread this butter mixture over the birds and leave them to marinate for 3–4 hours or until ready to cook.

4 Grill the poussins on the rack, breast side down, for 15 minutes or until the skin is well browned. Turn them over and cook for a further 20 minutes or until the flesh is cooked through. Test for doneness by pushing a skewer into the thickest part of the meat and any juices should run clear.

5 Serve with lemon wedges to squeeze over.

Thai chicken bites

If you prefer a spicier taste, use hot chilli sauce or fresh chilli puree instead of the sweet chilli sauce specified in the marinade for this recipe. Alternatively, one or two finely chopped and deseeded bird's-eye chillies could be added.

PREPARATION TIME: 15 MINUTES + MARINATING

COOKING TIME: 5 MINUTES

SERVES 4

675g (1½lb) chicken thighs or boneless breasts, skinned and
   cut into strips
1 tsp lemon grass purée
1 tsp ground coriander
1 tsp sweet chilli sauce
2 garlic cloves, peeled and crushed
100ml (4fl oz) coconut milk

TO SERVE
Thai fragrant rice
Stir-fried vegetables (see page 127)

1 Put the chicken strips in a bowl. Mix together the lemon grass purée, coriander, chilli sauce, garlic and coconut milk and pour over the chicken, turning the strips over until coated.

2 Leave to marinate for 3–4 hours or until ready to cook.

3 Thread the chicken strips on to skewers and grill on the rack for about 5 minutes until cooked, turning them over once and basting with the marinade left in the bowl.

tip

The marinade for this recipe would work equally well with prawns or white fish. Single prawns or pieces of chicken could be skewered on cocktail sticks and served as an appetizer with drinks.

Yakitori chicken sticks

These sweet, soy-glazed chicken skewers are one of Tokyo's most popular snacks, being sold to the city's hungry workers from 24-hour food bars and street stalls.

PREPARATION TIME: 10 MINUTES

COOKING TIME: LESS THAN 10 MINUTES

SERVES 4

100ml (4fl oz) dark soy sauce
2 Tbsp sake or dry sherry
2 Tbsp oil
1 tsp fresh ginger purée
2 Tbsp brown sugar
Freshly ground black pepper
8 boneless chicken thighs, skinned and cut into bite-sized pieces
1 green pepper, deseeded and cut into chunks
1 red pepper, deseeded and cut into chunks

1 In a bowl, whisk together the soy sauce, sake or sherry, oil, ginger and sugar until the sugar dissolves. Season with plenty of freshly ground black pepper.

2 Add the chicken, turning the pieces over until well coated, and leave to marinate for 2–3 hours or until ready to cook.

3 Thread the chicken and pepper chunks alternately on to skewers, pour the marinade left in the dish into a small pan and boil it on a conventional hob until it reduces by half.

4 Grill the chicken skewers on the rack for 6–8 minutes, turning over halfway and brushing with the reduced marinade so it forms a sticky glaze.

 ## tip

Instead of red and green peppers, chunks of spring onion can be threaded on to the skewers between the chicken pieces.

Chicken, olive and saffron tagine

Preserved lemons are often used in North African recipes such as this tagine, adding their own special tang to a dish. They are available in jars from larger supermarkets.

PREPARATION TIME: 20 MINUTES + PLUS STANDING

COOKING TIME: APPROX. 1 HOUR 20 MINUTES

SERVES 4

1 tsp ground turmeric
1 tsp ground ginger
1 tsp ground coriander
4 garlic cloves, peeled and crushed
4 chicken legs, skinned
1 onion, peeled and finely chopped
2 carrots, sliced
1 x 230g (8oz) tin chopped tomatoes
300ml (10fl oz) chicken stock
Pinch saffron threads
1 preserved lemon, sliced or chopped
100g (3½oz) olives
Salt and pepper

TO SERVE
Couscous

1 Mix together the turmeric, ginger, coriander and half the garlic and rub over the chicken pieces. Set aside for 30 minutes.

2 Put the remaining garlic, the onion, carrots, tomatoes and stock in a flameproof casserole or tagine dish, add the chicken pieces and crumble in the saffron.

3 Cover the casserole, or put the lid on the tagine dish, and cook on top of the chiminea for 1 hour.

4 Add the preserved lemon and olives and cook on top for a further 15–20 minutes until the chicken is very tender. Serve with couscous.

Five-spice chicken

Chinese five-spice powder is a blend of five and sometimes more, spices that are said to harmonize the yin and yang elements of a dish. Always included are star anise, fennel seeds, Szechwan peppercorns, cloves and cinnamon or cassia bark, with coriander, ginger and cardamom occasionally added as well. Jars of ready-mixed five-spice powder are available from supermarkets.

PREPARATION TIME: 10 MINUTES + MARINATING

PREPARATION TIME: 10 MINUTES + MARINATING

SERVES: 4

4 boneless chicken breasts, skin on
2 tsp Chinese five-spice powder
1 tsp garlic salt
1 tsp paprika
Juice of 2 limes
2 Tbsp sunflower oil

1 Cut several slashes through the thickest part of each chicken breast and place them in a dish. Mix together the five-spice powder, garlic salt and paprika and rub over the chicken. Pour over the lime juice and leave to marinate for 3–4 hours.

2 Brush the breasts with the oil and cook on the grill rack for about 15 minutes or until cooked through, turning over once or twice.

tip

If you find chicken breasts difficult to turn over on the grill rack, push two skewers through each breast about 5cm (2in) apart, threading several breasts on to each pair of skewers if they are long enough.

6 vegetarian dishes

Halloumi and felafel kebabs
Tofu, red pepper, mushroom and courgette satay
Tomatoes stuffed with mushrooms, pine nuts
  and bulghur wheat
Goat's cheese-stuffed mushrooms
Spicy bean burgers
Baked butternut squash with broccoli and
  cheese stuffing
Moroccan vegetable tagine
Stir-fried vegetables
Tangy vegetable kebabs
Roasted vegetables with pesto dressing
Aubergines stuffed with spicy couscous
Thai red vegetable curry
Glamorgan sausages
Fried halloumi with red onion, capers and olives
Aubergine, garlic and coriander mash on warm
  flatbreads

Halloumi and felafel kebabs

Halloumi, or hellim, cheese is a speciality of Cyprus, where in summer everyone cooks outside. This full-fat cheese is made from goat's milk, salt and a sprinkling of mint, and is firm enough to be cut into cubes and threaded on to kebab skewers. Tofu can be substituted for the cheese if you prefer.

PREPARATION TIME: 15 MINUTES

COOKING TIME: 5 MINUTES

SERVES 4

200g (7oz) halloumi cheese, cut into 2.5cm (1in) cubes
200g (7oz) firm vegetarian pâté of your choice, cut into 2.5cm (1in) cubes
8 felafel balls
1 green pepper, deseeded and cut into 2.5cm (1in) chunks
225g (8oz) mushrooms
4 Tbsp olive oil
Juice of 1/2 lemon
1 tsp fresh thyme leaves

TO SERVE
4 pitta breads or other flatbreads
6 Tbsp hummous
2 Tbsp olive oil
2 Tbsp chopped fresh parsley or coriander
1 lemon, cut into wedges

1 Thread the halloumi and vegetarian pâté cubes, felafel balls, green pepper pieces and mushrooms alternately on to eight skewers. Mix together the olive oil, lemon juice and thyme and brush over the kebabs.

2 Grill the kebabs for 5 minutes on the rack until the halloumi cheese and green pepper scorch and the other ingredients are heated through.

3 Warm the flatbreads as the kebabs cook. Spoon the hummous into a bowl, drizzle with the olive oil and sprinkle over the parsley or coriander. Serve the kebabs with lemon wedges to squeeze over, accompanied by the flatbreads and hummous.

Tofu, red pepper, mushroom and courgette satay

Made from cooked soya beans that have been ground, mixed with soya milk curds and pressed to drain off the whey, tofu is a high protein, low calorie food. Extremely versatile, it can be stir-fried, minced for burgers, braised in a sauce or cubed and threaded on to skewers for kebabs.

PREPARATION TIME: 15 MINUTES + MARINATING

COOKING TIME: 10 MINUTES

SERVES 4

250g (9oz) firm tofu, cut into 2.5cm (1in) cubes
4 Tbsp crunchy peanut butter
2 Tbsp Japanese soy sauce
200g (7oz) Greek yogurt
1 red pepper, deseeded and cut into chunks
12 button mushrooms
1 large or 2 small courgettes, cut into chunks
3 Tbsp sunflower oil

TO SERVE
Spicy tomato sauce (see page 163)

1 Place the cubes of tofu in a dish. Stir the peanut butter and soy sauce into the yogurt and spoon over the tofu, stirring until the cubes are coated. Leave to marinate for 1 hour or longer.

2 Thread the tofu, red pepper chunks, button mushrooms and courgette chunks alternately on to skewers and brush the vegetables with the oil.

3 Grill the satay for about 10 minutes, turning them over once or twice and brushing with any remaining marinade until browned. Serve hot.

 ## tip

Although bland when eaten on its own, tofu readily absorbs the flavours of other ingredients, making it a valuable ingredient in vegetarian dishes. Buy firm – sometimes called original – tofu for kebabs, which is available in packs from the chiller cabinet in larger supermarkets and health food stores.

Tomatoes stuffed with mushrooms, pine nuts and bulghur wheat

The suggested cooking time is only approximate as a lot will depend on the size and ripeness of the tomatoes. Keep an eye on them as they cook as they need to be mellow and tender but five minutes too long and they'll collapse.

PREPARATION TIME: 20 MINUTES + COOLING

COOKING TIME: 15 MINUTES

SERVES 4

4 ripe but firm beef tomatoes or 8 medium tomatoes
6 Tbsp bulghur wheat
Approx. 300ml (10fl oz) vegetable stock
2 Tbsp sun-dried tomato purée
2 Tbsp olive oil
1 shallot, peeled and chopped
1 garlic clove, peeled and finely chopped
115g (4oz) mushrooms, chopped
2 Tbsp toasted pine nuts

1 Cut the tops off the tomatoes and carefully scoop out the seeds, taking care not to split the skins. Turn the tomato cases upside down to drain.

2 Put the bulghur wheat in a heatproof bowl. Heat the stock with the tomato purée and, when boiling, pour over enough just to cover the wheat. Leave until the wheat grains absorb the stock and swell.

3 Heat the oil in a frying pan on a conventional hob and cook the shallots, garlic and mushrooms for 5 minutes. Remove from the heat, leave to cool, before stirring into the bulghur wheat with the pine nuts.

4 Spoon the stuffing into the tomatoes, packing it in, and replace the lids. Stand the tomatoes in a metal dish and cover with foil or a lid. Cook on the grill rack for 6–10 minutes or until the tomatoes are tender.

tip

Choose large, even-sized tomatoes that are ripe but still firm and blemish free.

Goat's cheese-stuffed mushrooms

French goat's cheeses tend to be stronger flavoured than British ones so buy whichever you prefer. If, like some people, you regard goat's cheese as the devil's work, substitute an ordinary soft cheese such as Boursin instead.

PREPARATION TIME: 15 MINUTES + MARINATING

COOKING TIME: LESS THAN 10 MINUTES

SERVES 4

8 large portobello mushrooms, stalks removed
4 Tbsp extra virgin olive oil
1 Tbsp lemon juice
2 garlic cloves, peeled and finely chopped
225g (8oz) soft goat's cheese
1 Tbsp snipped fresh chives
4 sun-dried tomatoes, finely chopped
3 Tbsp chopped fresh parsley

1 Place the mushrooms in a shallow dish. In another bowl mix together the olive oil, lemon juice and garlic and brush over the mushrooms, making sure they are evenly coated. Leave to marinate for 3–4 hours or until ready to cook.

2 Mix together the goat's cheese, chives and sun-dried tomatoes in a bowl.

3 Grill the mushrooms on the grill rack for about 5 minutes, starting them off rounded side up, then turning them over once or twice, until tender.

4 Remove the mushrooms from the rack and place on a baking sheet. Spoon the goat's cheese mixture into the centre of each mushroom and stand the baking sheet on the rack. Cook for about 1 minute until the cheese starts to melt. Serve at once, sprinkled with the parsley.

 ## tip

These could be served as a starter with a salad garnish or with grilled vegetables as a main meal. There's no need to peel the mushrooms first, just wipe the caps with a clean damp cloth.

Spicy bean burgers

Vegetarians can feel left out at barbecues, but these tasty burgers should redress the balance.

PREPARATION TIME: 20 MINUTES + PLUS CHILLING

COOKING TIME: 20 MINUTES

MAKES 6

2 Tbsp olive oil plus extra for brushing
1 onion, peeled and chopped
1 Tbsp ground coriander
1 tsp ground ginger
2 garlic cloves, peeled and crushed
1 tsp Marmite
2 carrots, grated
1 x 400g (14oz) tin red kidney beans, drained and rinsed
3 Tbsp chopped fresh coriander
1 egg, beaten
100g (3^1/$_2$oz) fresh breadcrumbs
Salt and freshly ground black pepper

TO SERVE
Lettuce, tomato slices and onion rings
Spicy tomato sauce (see page 163)
Avocado mayonnaise (see page 150)

1 Heat the oil in a frying pan on a conventional hob and fry the onion for 5 minutes. Add the coriander, ginger and garlic and cook for a further 5 minutes or until the onion has softened. Remove from the heat and leave to cool.

2 Tip the onion mixture into a food processor, add the Marmite, carrots, kidney beans and fresh coriander and process until the beans have been reduced to a coarse meal and everything is well blended.

3 Transfer the mixture to a bowl and stir in the egg, breadcrumbs and seasoning. Shape the mixture into six round, flat cakes and chill for 3–4 hours or longer to firm up.

4 Brush with olive oil and cook on the grill rack for about 5 minutes on each side until golden brown.

Baked butternut squash with broccoli and cheese stuffing

This is a great vegetarian dish that can be prepared in advance and then reheated by wrapping the squash halves in foil and placing them on top of the chiminea, while steaks and burgers for meat eaters sizzle on the rack below.

PREPARATION TIME: 30 MINUTES

COOKING TIME: 1 HOUR

SERVES 2

1 butternut squash, weighing approx. 700g (1¹/₂lb)
2 Tbsp olive oil
Freshly ground black pepper

STUFFING
50g (2oz) butter
50g (2oz) mushrooms, sliced
¹/₄ red pepper, deseeded and chopped
115g (4oz) small broccoli florets
¹/₂ thick-sliced bread, cut into 5mm (¹/₄in) cubes
75g (3oz) grated Cheddar cheese
2 Tbsp chopped fresh parsley

1 Cut the squash in half lengthways and remove the seeds and fibres from the centre. Score the flesh in a criss-cross pattern with a sharp knife and brush with the olive oil. Season with pepper, wrap each half in foil and grill on the rack for about 40 minutes or until tender.

2 To make the stuffing, heat the butter in a frying pan on a conventional hob and fry the mushrooms, red pepper and broccoli florets for 5 minutes. Add the bread cubes and fry for a further 5 minutes. Remove from the heat and stir in half the cheese and half the parsley.

3 Unwrap the squash and spoon out the flesh from each half, taking care not to split the skins. Add the flesh to the frying pan and place the hollowed out skins on separate sheets of fresh foil.

4 Fill the skins with the stuffing, pressing it down lightly and piling it up as necessary. Sprinkle over the rest of the cheese and the parsley, wrap the foil around to make loose parcels and warm through on the rack for 10 minutes or on top of the chiminea for 25–30 minutes before serving.

Moroccan vegetable tagine

Harissa is a fiery chilli condiment from North Africa. It can be added before cooking, or served on the side for diners to stir in themselves, but remember, a little goes a long way!

PREPARATION TIME: 20 MINUTES

COOKING TIME: 1¼ HOURS

SERVES 4

2 Tbsp oil
1 large onion, peeled and chopped
2 carrots, sliced
2 medium potatoes, peeled and cut into chunks
1 Tbsp ground coriander
1 tsp paprika
Pinch saffron threads, soaked in a little hot water for 5 minutes
1 butternut squash, peeled, deseeded and cut into 2.5cm (1in) chunks
2 courgettes, thickly sliced
1 x 400g (14oz) tin chopped tomatoes
300ml (10fl oz) vegetable stock
1 x 400g (14oz) tin chickpeas, drained and rinsed
3 Tbsp raisins
1 tsp harissa paste, or to taste
Salt and pepper

TO SERVE
Couscous

1 Heat the oil in a cast-iron casserole on a conventional hob, add the onion, carrots and potatoes and fry for 10 minutes. Add the coriander and paprika and fry for 1 minute more.

2 Add the saffron and its soaking water, the squash, courgettes, tomatoes and stock. Cover the casserole and cook on top of the chiminea for 45 minutes.

3 Stir in the chickpeas, raisins, harissa paste and seasoning then cook, uncovered, for a further 15 minutes or until the vegetables are tender and the cooking juices have reduced and thickened. Serve with couscous.

Stir-fried vegetables

Any combination of vegetables can be stir-fried but they need to be cut into similar-sized pieces, and firmer vegetables such as carrots and onions that take longer to cook, added to the wok first.

PREPARATION TIME: 15 MINUTES

COOKING TIME: 10 MINUTES

SERVES 2

2 Tbsp oil
1 red onion, peeled and thinly sliced
1 carrot, peeled and cut into matchsticks
1 red pepper, deseeded and thinly sliced
1 yellow pepper, deseeded and thinly sliced
50g (2oz) mange tout, cut in half lengthways
115g (4oz) baby corn, cut in half lengthways
85g (3oz) bean sprouts
1 x 150g (5oz) sachet straight-to-wok noodles
3 Tbsp light soy sauce
1 tsp sweet chilli sauce

1 Heat the oil in a wok on top of the chiminea, add the onion and carrot and stir-fry for 3 minutes. Add the peppers and stir-fry for a further 3 minutes.

2 Add the mange tout, baby corn and bean sprouts and stir-fry for 2 minutes, then add the noodles and mix with the vegetables.

3 Add the soy and sweet chilli sauces and stir-fry for 2 minutes, tossing the noodles and vegetables together so they are well coated.

tip

The vegetables can be stir-fried on their own or tossed with noodles, as in this recipe, for a more substantial dish.If you prefer to buy dried noodles, allow about 100g (3½oz) for two people and cook them according to the packet instructions before adding to the wok.

Tangy vegetable kebabs

Make sure all the vegetable pieces are well coated with the soy-sauce mix before you place them on the grill rack, otherwise dry items like aubergine and courgette chunks will become chewy and unpleasant to eat.

PREPARATION TIME: 10 MINUTES

COOKING TIME: 5 MINUTES

SERVES 4

1 red pepper, deseeded and cut into 2.5cm (1in) pieces
$1/2$ red onion, peeled cut into chunks and the layers separated
1 courgette, cut into 2cm ($3/4$in) slices
1 small aubergine, cut into small chunks
115g (4oz) button mushrooms
2 Tbsp light soy sauce
1 Tbsp soft brown sugar
1 tsp Dijon mustard
1 Tbsp oil
1 tsp chopped fresh marjoram or oregano

TO SERVE
Lemon wedges
Spicy tomato sauce (see page 163)
Guacamole (see page 153)
Pitta breads

1 Thread the vegetable pieces alternately on to 4 large or 8 small skewers.

2 Mix together the soy sauce, brown sugar, mustard, oil and marjoram or oregano and brush over the vegetables.

3 Cook on the grill rack for about 5 minutes or until the vegetables are tender and starting to scorch at the edges.

4 Serve the kebabs with lemon wedges to squeeze over and accompany with spicy tomato sauce, guacamole and warm pitta breads.

Roasted vegetables with pesto dressing

The pesto dressing in this recipe gives roasted vegetables a fresh herby twist.

PREPARATION TIME: 15 MINUTES

COOKING TIME: 15 MINUTES

SERVES 4

2 red peppers, deseeded and quartered
2 yellow peppers, deseeded and quartered
4 Tbsp olive oil
1 aubergine, cut into thin slices lengthways
2 courgettes, cut into thin slices lengthways
4 plum tomatoes, halved
1 large red onion, peeled and cut into 8 wedges

DRESSING
25g (1oz) fresh basil leaves, roughly chopped
2 garlic cloves, peeled and crushed
2 Tbsp pine nuts or chopped almonds
Finely grated rind and juice of 1 lemon
5 Tbsp extra virgin olive oil
Freshly ground black pepper

1 Cook the pepper quarters on the grill rack for about 10 minutes or until they are tender and the skins charred. Remove from the grill and place on a sheet of foil. Wrap the foil around the peppers to make a tightly sealed parcel and leave until cool enough to handle. Unwrap the peppers and pull off the skins.

2 While the peppers are cooling, brush the olive oil over the aubergine slices, courgette slices, tomato halves and red-onion wedges and grill on the rack until tender. The aubergine, courgette and red onion will take about 5 minutes, the tomato halves will only need about 1 minute or they will collapse. As they cook, pile the vegetables into a serving dish.

3 To make the dressing, whizz all the ingredients together in a liquidizer, or grind the basil, garlic and nuts to a paste by hand using a pestle and mortar, and then gradually work in the lemon juice and oil.

4 Spoon the dressing over the vegetables and serve while they are still warm.

Aubergines stuffed with spicy couscous

If you want to spice this dish up even more add to the stuffing a teaspoon of harissa – a fiery chilli condiment from North Africa made by pounding red chillies with garlic and spices such as caraway, cumin and coriander. Unlike some chilli condiments it has a salty rather than sweet flavour so you may need to add a pinch of sugar or spoonful of honey as well.

PREPARATION TIME: 30 MINUTES

COOKING TIME 1 HOUR 20 MINUTES

SERVES 4

2 large aubergines
4 Tbsp olive oil
4 shallots, peeled and chopped
115g (4oz) mushrooms, sliced
1 tsp paprika
1 Tbsp ground coriander
225g (8oz) couscous
600ml (1pt) vegetable stock
2 Tbsp tomato purée
50g (2oz) lightly toasted pine nuts or cashews
50g (2oz) sultanas
4 Tbsp chopped fresh coriander
Freshly ground black pepper
8 Tbsp grated Cheddar or other hard cheese

TO SERVE
Green salad

1 Cut the aubergines in half lengthways, leaving the stalks attached. Cut the flesh out of the centre of each half, leaving a 5mm (1/4in) border to support the skin and taking care not to split the skin. Chop the flesh finely.

2 Heat the oil in a large frying pan and fry the shallots over a low heat for 5 minutes. Add the mushrooms, paprika, ground coriander and aubergine flesh and fry for another 5 minutes, stirring occasionally.

3 Add the couscous, stock and tomato purée and bring to the boil. Reduce the heat and simmer gently for about 10 minutes or until the couscous has absorbed all the liquid.

4 Remove from the heat and stir in the nuts, sultanas, coriander and pepper. Leave to cool.

5 Place each aubergine half on a sheet of foil and fill with the couscous stuffing, packing it in tightly. Top with the grated cheese and wrap the foil around the aubergines in a loose parcel, folding over the edges of the foil to make a tight seal.

6 Cook the aubergines on the grill rack for about 1 hour or until tender. Serve hot with green salad.

tip

The stuffing can be prepared using the top of the chiminea or a conventional hob as you prefer. If you don't have pine nuts or cashews in your store cupboard, flaked almonds or chopped hazelnuts would work equally well.

Thai red vegetable curry

Made from salted, fermented fish or prawns and used in Thai recipes in much the same way as soy sauce is used in China, fish sauce adds its own special savoury tang to dishes. It keeps well and doesn't need to be refrigerated after opening. If you prefer not to use fish sauce substitute dark soy sauce instead.

PREPARATION TIME: 20 MINUTES

COOKING TIME: ABOUT 45 MINUTES

SERVES 4

2 Tbsp oil
2 Tbsp Thai red curry paste
1 large onion, peeled and sliced
1 large carrot, thinly sliced or chopped into small cubes
2 sweet potatoes, peeled and cut into 2cm (¾in) chunks
1 green pepper, deseeded and chopped
1 courgette, sliced
115g (4oz) mushrooms, sliced or quartered
2 Tbsp Thai fish sauce (nam pla)
Juice of 1 lime
2 tsp brown sugar
1 tsp lemon grass purée
350ml (12fl oz) coconut milk

1 Heat the oil in a large heavy pan on top of the chiminea, add the curry paste, onion and carrot and fry for 2–3 minutes until the onion begins to soften.

2 Add the sweet potatoes and fry for a further 10 minutes, stirring occasionally. Add the green pepper, courgette and mushrooms, fry for 2 minutes, then add the fish sauce, lime juice, sugar, lemon grass purée and coconut milk.

3 Cover the pan and simmer the curry for 20–30 minutes or until the vegetables are tender.

tip

Add extra curry paste if you like things hot, and vary the vegetables according to what you have available. Cut slow-cooking ones like carrots and potatoes into small pieces or blanch them first in a pan of boiling water for 5 minutes.

Glamorgan sausages

Not sausages that carnivores would recognize, but a tasty blend of breadcrumbs, leek, cheese and parsley for vegetarians to enjoy. This recipe adds tofu, mushrooms and sweet potatoes to the traditional mix.

PREPARATION TIME: 25 MINUTES + CHILLING

COOKING TIME: 15 MINUTES

SERVES 4

2 Tbsp olive oil plus extra for brushing
1 leek, trimmed, halved lengthways and finely sliced
2 portobello mushrooms, very finely chopped
200g (7oz) firm tofu, grated
225g (8oz) sweet potatoes, boiled and mashed
75g (3oz) mature Cheddar cheese, grated
75g (3oz) fresh wholemeal breadcrumbs
2 tsp wholegrain mustard
3 Tbsp chopped fresh parsley
Freshly ground black pepper
50g (2oz) plain flour

1 Heat 2 Tbsp olive oil in a pan and fry the leek and mushrooms on a conventional hob for 5 minutes until softened. Transfer to a bowl and stir in the tofu, sweet potatoes, cheese, breadcrumbs, mustard, parsley and black pepper.

2 Shape the mixture into eight sausages and chill for 3–4 hours to firm them up.

3 Roll the sausages in the flour and brush all over with olive oil. Cook on a hot plate or griddle on the rack for about 10 minutes or until the sausages are golden brown all over.

tip

Vegetarians needn't miss out when sausages are on the menu, as they can enjoy these veggie bangers. As the "sausages" have no skins to keep them in shape, they need to be chilled for several hours so they firm up and it's probably better to cook them on a hot plate on the rack rather than directly on the rack itself so there's no danger of them breaking up and falling into the coals.

Fried halloumi with red onion, capers and olives

The sharpness of red onion, capers and olives contrasts well with the mild flavour of the halloumi cheese. Take care when cutting the block into slices as the cheese can sometimes split in half.

PREPARATION TIME: 10 MINUTES

COOKING TIME: LESS THAN 5 MINUTES

SERVES 4

5 Tbsp olive oil
1 small red onion, peeled and finely chopped
1 Tbsp capers
Juice of ½ lemon
1 garlic clove, peeled and finely chopped
1 tsp Dijon mustard
115g (4oz) black olives
1 x 250g (9oz) pack halloumi cheese, cut into 5mm (¼in) slices
3 Tbsp plain flour

1 Mix 3 Tbsp olive oil with the red onion, capers, lemon juice, garlic and mustard. Add the olives and set aside.

2 Dust the halloumi slices with the flour and brush with the remaining olive oil.

3 Fry the cheese on a hot griddle pan on the grill rack for 1–2 minutes on each side until the slices are golden.

4 Drain on kitchen paper and divide between serving plates. Spoon over the dressing and serve while the cheese is still warm.

tip

Make sure the griddle pan is really hot before you add the cheese slices so they brown quickly without melting too much. Have the dressing ready to pour over the cooked cheese straight away. If you prefer, the dish can be made with slices of firm tofu instead of halloumi.

Aubergine, garlic and coriander mash on warm flatbreads

As well as making a satisfying vegetarian dish, this mash can also be served as an accompaniment to roast lamb or pork kebabs, or spooned on to small squares of toast and served as an appetizer with drinks. Grilling the aubergines directly over the heat gives them a deliciously smoky flavour.

PREPARATION TIME: 15 MINUTES

COOKING TIME: LESS THAN 15 MINUTES

SERVES 6

2 large aubergines
1 thick slice of bread (any sort), torn or cut into small pieces
3 large garlic cloves, peeled and chopped
1 Tbsp lemon juice
4 Tbsp extra virgin olive oil
4 Tbsp chopped fresh coriander
Salt and freshly ground black pepper
6 flatbreads or pitta breads

TO SERVE
Cherry tomatoes, halved
Cucumber slices

1 Cook the whole aubergines directly on the grill rack for about 10 minutes, turning them over regularly. They are done when the flesh feels soft when a skewer is pushed through the middle, and the skin comes away easily.

2 When the aubergines are cool enough to handle, cut them in half lengthways and scoop out the flesh into a food processor. Add the bread, garlic, lemon juice and olive oil and whizz until smooth and creamy. If you don't have a food processor, mash the aubergine flesh and gradually beat in the other ingredients.

3 Transfer the mixture to a bowl, stir in the coriander and season to taste.

4 Lightly toast the flatbreads on the grill rack and serve topped with the aubergine mash. Accompany with cherry tomato halves and cucumber slices.

7 salads and vegetable accompaniments

Mixed bean bowl
Watermelon, feta and orange salad
Roasted sweet potato wedges
Coleslaw
Jacket potatoes
Chickpea tabbouleh
New potato salad with bacon, rocket and
   spring onions
Apricot and nut couscous
Layered summer salad
Panzanella
Calypso rice salad

Note
These dishes need to be prepared in advance,
and are not all prepared on the chiminea.

Mixed bean bowl

This colourful bean bowl has lots of interesting textures and flavours, making it a great accompaniment to plainly grilled meat or fish. It can also be served on its own as a vegetarian dish with lots of crusty bread.

PREPARATION TIME: 15 MINUTES

COOKING TIME: 10 MINUTES

SERVES 4

175g (6oz) shelled broad beans
115g (4oz) green beans, trimmed and cut into short lengths
1 yellow pepper, deseeded and finely chopped
1 red pepper, deseeded and finely chopped
9 cherry tomatoes, halved or quartered
1 x 400g (14oz) tin cannellini beans, drained and rinsed
6 Tbsp extra virgin olive oil
2–3 Tbsp balsamic vinegar, depending on strength
2 garlic cloves, peeled and crushed
Salt and freshly ground black pepper
6 large basil leaves, torn

1 If the broad beans are frozen, cook them according to the packet instructions on a conventional hob. If they are fresh, bring a pan of water to the boil, add the beans and cook for 10 minutes or until tender. Drain, cool under cold water and peel off the beans' white outer skins if you prefer.

2 Cook the green beans in a pan of boiling water on the hob for 2 minutes, either adding them to the broad beans towards the end of their cooking time or in a separate pan. Drain and cool under cold water.

3 Pat the broad beans and green beans dry with kitchen paper and put in a serving dish with the yellow pepper, red pepper, cherry tomatoes and cannellini beans.

4 Whisk together the oil, vinegar, garlic and seasoning and pour into the dish, tossing the beans and vegetables lightly together to coat them in the dressing. Serve with the basil leaves scattered over.

 ## tip

It's best to tear fresh basil with your hands rather than chop it with a knife, so you don't bruise the delicate leaves and spoil their flavour.

Watermelon, feta and orange salad

Colourful, light and refreshing, this summer salad should be made several hours ahead without the rocket and left in a covered bowl in the refrigerator so the fruit and cheese absorb the dressing. The sweet flavour and crisp texture of the watermelon is the perfect foil for the sharp-flavoured feta cheese.

PREPARATION TIME: 15 MINUTES

SERVES 6

$^1/_2$ medium-sized watermelon
2 seedless oranges
200g (7oz) feta cheese
100g (3$^1/_2$oz) rocket leaves

DRESSING
150ml ($^1/_4$ pt) light olive oil
1 tsp clear honey
3 Tbsp white wine vinegar
Salt and pepper
1 pomegranate (optional)

1 Cut the watermelon into wedges, remove the skin and deseed, if necessary. Peel and segment the oranges and crumble the feta or cut into small cubes. Rinse the rocket, shake well to remove excess water and keep in the refrigerator in a sealed plastic bag until needed.

2 To make the dressing, whisk together the olive oil, honey, vinegar and seasoning. Cut the pomegranate in half, if using, pick out the seeds with a skewer or pointed knife and add them to the dressing.

3 Put the melon, orange segments and feta in a serving bowl and pour over the dressing. Cover with clingfilm and refrigerate for several hours.

4 When ready to serve, toss the rocket leaves gently into the salad.

 tip

Cubes of watermelon and feta speared on toothpicks make good appetizers.

Roasted sweet potato wedges

If you want to bake the sweet potatoes whole instead of in wedges, scrub them, prick all over with a fork and wrap in a double thickness of foil. Push them into the embers or place on the grill rack and cook for 35–40 minutes until tender when pierced with a skewer.

PREPARATION TIME: 15 MINUTES + MARINATING

COOKING TIME: LESS THAN 20 MINUTES

SERVES 6

3 medium-sized sweet potatoes
6 Tbsp olive oil
1 tsp fresh garlic purée
4 Tbsp orange juice
1 Tbsp finely chopped fresh rosemary

TO SERVE
Soured cream
Guacamole (see page 153)

1 Scrub the sweet potatoes, pat dry with kitchen paper and cut into thick wedges.

2 Cook the wedges in a pan of boiling water on a conventional hob for 6–7 minutes or until just tender when pierced with a skewer. Drain and dry the wedges on kitchen paper or a clean tea towel.

3 In a bowl, mix together the olive oil, garlic purée, orange juice and rosemary. Add the still warm wedges, turning them over so they are well coated. Leave to marinate for 5–6 hours or overnight.

4 Lift the wedges from the marinade and grill on the rack for about 5 minutes on each side until tender and lightly scorched, basting with any leftover marinade as they cook.

 ## tip

Wedges of butternut squash or pumpkin could also be cooked in the same way, but scoop out and discard the seeds and fibres first.

Coleslaw

This recipe is a colourful combination of white and red cabbage, with carrot and celery added for extra crunch. A flavoured mayonnaise could be used if you wish (choose whichever takes your fancy from the suggestions on page 150).

PREPARATION TIME: 20 MINUTES

SERVES 8

1/4 head white cabbage, core removed and leaves finely shredded
1/4 head red cabbage, core removed and leaves finely shredded
1 large carrot, coarsely grated
2 celery sticks, sliced
2 Tbsp chopped fresh parsley
6 Tbsp mayonnaise
Salt and pepper
Juice of 1/2 lemon
75g (3oz) sultanas
3 Tbsp chopped pecans
1 shallot, peeled and finely chopped (optional)

1 Combine the shredded white and red cabbage, carrot and celery in a large bowl.

2 Mix together the parsley, mayonnaise, seasoning and lemon juice and toss with the vegetables in the bowl until they are lightly coated.

3 Add the chopped shallot and stir it in just before serving. Then sprinkle over the sultanas and pecans.

 tip

If you like onion in your coleslaw, don't add it too early as, if left to stand too long, the acid in the onion will give the coleslaw an unpleasantly sour taste and it could even start to ferment.

Jacket potatoes

You can speed up the cooking of these by microwaving the potatoes on full power for about 15 minutes until they are tender and then finishing them on the grill rack to crisp their the skins.

PREPARATION TIME: 5 MINUTES

COOKING TIME: ABOUT 1¼ HOURS

SERVES 4

4 large even-sized potatoes

TO SERVE
Butter
Soured cream and chives
Filling of your choice (see suggestions in step 3)

1 Scrub the potatoes and pat dry with kitchen paper. Prick the skins all over with a fork or score around the middle of each potato with a sharp knife.

2 Wrap the potatoes in double thicknesses of foil and either push them into the glowing coals at the bottom of the chiminea, or stand them on the grill rack. Cook for about 1¼ hours or until the potatoes are tender when pierced with a skewer.

3 Unwrap the potatoes, cut a cross in the top of each or slice in half and serve topped with butter or soured cream and snipped fresh chives. More substantial fillings could be baked beans and sausages, grated cheese and chopped ham or chopped chicken with avocado and cherry tomatoes dressed with mayonnaise.

tip

If you prefer your jacket potatoes to have crispy skins, cook them in the foil until they are just tender, then unwrap and finish off on the grill rack, turning them over regularly so the skins crisp and scorch a little.

Chickpea tabbouleh

Tabbouleh is a bulghur wheat and herb salad popular in the Middle East, where it is served as a mezze or accompaniment to grilled meat or chicken. This version is made more substantial by the addition of chickpeas and chopped tomatoes.

PREPARATION TIME: 10 MINUTES + STANDING

SERVES 6

175g (6oz) bulghur wheat
Freshly ground black pepper
2 Tbsp chopped fresh coriander
2 Tbsp chopped fresh mint
2 Tbsp chopped fresh parsley
3 tomatoes, finely diced
1 x 400g (14oz) tin chickpeas, drained and rinsed
Juice of 1 lemon
3 Tbsp olive oil

1 Put the bulghur wheat in a heatproof bowl, season with pepper and pour over enough boiling water to just cover the grains. Put a plate on top of the bowl and leave to stand for 20 minutes until the water has been absorbed.

2 Fork up the grains, before stirring in the herbs, tomatoes and chickpeas. Squeeze over the lemon juice and drizzle with the olive oil, then toss until well combined.

 tip

If you don't want to buy three different herbs, you could just add parsley to the bulghur wheat. It's important to use fresh herbs as dried ones have too strong a taste.

New potato salad with bacon, rocket and spring onions

It's not necessary to peel the potatoes in this recipe, simply scrub them with a soft brush under cold water to remove any mud or loose bits of skin.

PREPARATION TIME: 15 MINUTES + COOLING

COOKING TIME: 20 MINUTES

SERVES 6

900g (2lb) baby new potatoes
6 Tbsp extra virgin olive oil
2 Tbsp balsamic vinegar
2 garlic cloves, peeled and crushed
1 tsp Dijon mustard
1 Tbsp finely chopped fresh parsley
Salt and freshly ground black pepper
6 thin rashers streaky bacon
4 spring onions, chopped
50g (2oz) rocket

1 Bring a large pan of water to the boil, add the potatoes and boil for 10 minutes or until tender.

2 In a serving bowl, whisk together the olive oil, balsamic vinegar, garlic, mustard, parsley and seasoning. Drain the cooked potatoes and add to the bowl straight away, turning the potatoes over so they are coated in the dressing. Set aside to cool.

3 Grill or dry-fry the bacon rashers until crisp. Drain and chop or break into small pieces. Scatter over the potatoes with the onions.

4 Add the rocket leaves to the salad just before serving.

tip

Pouring the dressing over the potatoes while they're still warm means they'll absorb all its flavour as they cool. The potatoes, bacon and onions can be prepared well ahead, but add the rocket just before serving so the leaves don't wilt.

Apricot and nut couscous

Instant couscous needs no pre-cooking, just soaking in a bowl of hot stock so the grains swell and become soft. Preserved lemons can be bought in jars in larger supermarkets but if you can't find them, either leave them out or stir in the finely grated rind of a fresh lemon with the other ingredients.

PREPARATION TIME: 15 MINUTES + PLUS STANDING

COOKING TIME: LESS THAN 10 MINUTES

SERVES 6

50g (2oz) butter
2 Tbsp oil
2 tsp ground coriander
1 tsp ground cinnamon
4 shallots or large spring onions, peeled and roughly chopped
115g (4oz) ready-to-eat dried apricots, chopped
75g (3oz) shelled pistachios
75g (3oz) toasted flaked almonds
Approx. 1L (1³/4 pt) chicken or vegetable stock
1 tsp harissa paste
500g (1lb 2oz) instant couscous
1 preserved lemon, finely chopped
2 Tbsp chopped fresh mint
Salt and freshly ground black pepper

1 Heat the butter and oil in a pan on a conventional hob and add the coriander and cinnamon. Fry gently for 1 minute, then add the shallots or spring onions, apricots, pistachios and almonds and fry for 5 minutes, stirring occasionally.

2 Bring the stock to the boil on the hob and stir in the harissa. Put the couscous in a large heatproof bowl, pour over the hot stock, cover and leave for 5 minutes until the couscous has absorbed all the liquid.

3 Fluff up the grains of couscous with a fork and stir in the apricot mixture from the frying pan, the chopped lemon, mint and seasoning.

Layered summer salad

Make this salad in a clear glass or plastic bowl so diners can see all the colourful layers. Other ingredients can be substituted for the ones used here, so layer up your favourites in whatever order you please.

PREPARATION TIME: 20 MINUTES

COOKING TIME: 5 MINUTES

SERVES 4–6

3 rashers streaky bacon
$1/2$ iceberg lettuce, shredded
115g (4oz) button or chestnut mushrooms, thinly sliced
115g (4oz) grated Cheddar cheese
1 x 200g (7oz) tin sweetcorn with peppers, drained
$1/4$ cucumber, sliced
3 spring onions, trimmed and finely sliced
8 Tbsp garlic and lemon mayonnaise (see page 150)
2 Tbsp natural yogurt
2 tsp Dijon mustard
1 large tomato, cut into wedges
2 Tbsp chopped fresh parsley

1 Grill the bacon for about 5 minutes until crisp. Leave to cool, then chop into small pieces.

2 In a large class or plastic salad bowl, layer up the lettuce, mushrooms, cheese, sweetcorn, cucumber and spring onions.

3 Mix together the mayonnaise, yogurt and mustard until smooth and spoon over the salad. Cover with clingfilm and chill until ready to serve.

4 Arrange the tomato wedges on top of the salad and scatter over the bacon and parsley.

tip

If making this salad for vegetarians, omit the bacon and replace it with grated or finely diced courgette and carrot or small sprigs of watercress.

Panzanella

Every Tuscan cook has their own version of this popular Italian salad but, as well as good country bread, most include tomatoes and lots of fresh herbs. The salad needs to be made about 1 hour ahead so the bread can absorb the flavours of the dressing, but don't prepare it any more in advance than this or the bread will go soggy.

PREPARATION TIME: 15 MINUTES + COOLING AND STANDING

COOKING TIME: 5 MINUTES

SERVES: 6

4 thick slices of country bread, 2–3 days old
10 Tbsp extra virgin olive oil
1 red onion, peeled and finely sliced
1 small ridge cucumber, chopped
6 plum ripe tomatoes, quartered
2 garlic cloves, peeled and coarsely crushed
1 Tbsp white wine vinegar
1 Tbsp balsamic vinegar
Salt and freshly ground black pepper
2 Tbsp capers, rinsed, or 12 caperberries
2 Tbsp chopped fresh flat leaf parsley
2 Tbsp torn basil leaves

1 Brush each slice of bread with a tablespoon of the olive oil and toast or cook in a heavy frying pan until golden on both sides.

2 Cool the bread and either tear into chunks or cut into small pieces.

3 Place the bread in a serving dish and add the onion slices, chopped cucumber and tomato halves.

4 Whisk together the rest of the olive oil with the garlic, wine vinegar, balsamic vinegar and seasoning and pour over the salad. Leave to stand for 1 hour.

5 Add the capers or caperberries, parsley and basil and serve.

Calypso rice salad

Serve this rice salad either warm or cold as an accompaniment to roast chicken, roast pork or grilled seafood. If you want it to be a vegetarian dish, use vegetable stock instead of chicken.

PREPARATION TIME: 15 MINUTES

COOKING TIME: ABOUT 40 MINUTES

SERVES 4

2 Tbsp oil
1 red onion, peeled and chopped
1 tsp ground turmeric
1 tsp ground coriander
$1/2$ red pepper, deseeded and chopped
250g (9oz) long-grain rice
700ml (1$1/4$ pt) chicken stock
175g (6oz) frozen peas
1 pineapple ring, chopped into small pieces
$1/2$ papaya, peeled, deseeded and diced
2 Tbsp chopped fresh parsley or coriander

1 Heat the oil in a wok or large frying pan on a conventional hob and fry the onion until softened. Sprinkle in the turmeric and coriander and fry for 1 minute.

2 Stir in the red pepper and rice and pour in 600ml (1pt) of the stock. Leave to simmer for 10 minutes.

3 Stir in the peas and cook for a further 10–15 minutes or until the rice is tender, adding the remaining stock as necessary and stirring from time to time to stop the rice from sticking.

4 Stir in the pineapple, papaya and parsley or coriander and cook for 2–3 minutes until heated through.

tip

To ring the changes with this recipe, use long grain and wild rice (available ready mixed in packets) or nutty wholegrain rice instead of plain white. If using wholegrain, you'll need to increase the cooking time to around 20–30 minutes, but be guided by the packet instructions.

8 Pickles, dressings, dips and salsas

Flavoured butters
Flavoured mayonnaises
Sweet chilli dipping sauce
Piccalilli
Guacamole
Romesco sauce
Blue cheese and chive dressing
Cream cheese and sun-blushed tomato dip
Spicy peanut dipping sauce
Tzatziki
Cucumber, carrot and white radish relish
Pepper, tomato and sweetcorn relish
Avocado, pineapple and kidney bean salsa
Mango, red onion and cucumber salsa
Spicy tomato sauce

Flavoured butters

Using these flavoured butters is an easy way to liven up plainly grilled meat, fish or chicken or a jacket potato. The butters can be prepared well in advance and kept in the refrigerator or frozen until needed, just like ordinary butter. But bear in mind that the flavours will get stronger the longer they are stored so, as a guide, keep them for up to 3 days in the fridge, or 1 month in the freezer. Use salted or unsalted butter according to personal preference.

To prepare, let the butter come to room temperature so it softens and then mash it with a fork until smooth. Work in your chosen flavourings until they are evenly combined with the butter and spoon on to a small sheet of clingfilm or greaseproof paper. Shape into a log and roll the film or paper around the butter, twisting the ends tightly so the log keeps its shape. Chill until firm, then unwrap and cut the butter into rounds to serve.

BLUE CHEESE AND WALNUT BUTTER
Mash 150g (5oz) unsalted butter – the Blue Cheese is salty – with 150g (5oz) crumbled Gorgonzola cheese and 25g (1oz) finely chopped walnuts.

FRESH HERB AND GARLIC BUTTER
Mash 175g (6oz) butter with 2 Tbsp chopped fresh parsley, 2 Tbsp snipped fresh chives and 2 large garlic cloves, peeled and crushed.

ORANGE AND TARRAGON BUTTER
Mash 175g (6oz) butter with the finely grated rind of 1 large orange and 2 Tbsp chopped fresh tarragon.

ANCHOVY AND CAPER BUTTER
Mash 175g (6oz) butter with 6 finely chopped anchovy fillets, 2 tsp chopped capers, 1 tsp Dijon mustard and the juice of 1/2 lemon.

GINGER AND LEMON GRASS BUTTER
Mash 175g (6oz) butter with 1 tsp fresh ginger purée and 1 tsp fresh lemon grass purée.

TOMATO AND CORNICHON BUTTER
Mash 175g (6oz) butter with 3 finely chopped sun-blushed tomatoes, 6 finely chopped baby gherkins (cornichons) and 2 tsp lemon juice.

Flavoured mayonnaises

These can be served as a dip for kebabs or Sweet potato wedges (see page 137) or to accompany steaks, chops, chicken, fish or jacket potatoes.

AVOCADO MAYONNAISE

Mash the flesh of 1 avocado with 1 Tbsp lemon juice and stir into 175ml (6fl oz) mayonnaise. Sprinkle with finely snipped fresh chives.

DILL AND HORSERADISH MAYONNAISE

Stir 2 Tbsp finely chopped fresh dill and 2 tsp creamed horseradish into 175ml (6fl oz) mayonnaise.

TOMATO CHILLI MAYONNAISE

Deseed and very finely chop 1 large red chilli and stir into 175ml (6fl oz) mayonnaise with 2 Tbsp tomato ketchup.

ORANGE AND BASIL MAYONNAISE

Stir the finely grated rind and juice of 1 small orange into 175ml (6fl oz) mayonnaise with 1 Tbsp finely shredded fresh basil leaves.

GARLIC AND LEMON MAYONNAISE

Peel and crush 2 large garlic cloves and stir into 175ml (6fl oz) mayonnaise with the finely grated rind and juice of 1 lemon.

CURRIED MAYONNAISE

Stir 2 tsp curry paste and 1 Tbsp mango chutney into 175ml (6fl oz) mayonnaise. Sprinkle with finely chopped fresh coriander.

Sweet chilli dipping sauce

Peppadew are small piquant peppers that claim to give a little bite rather than going for the full burn. Sold in 375g jars, they can be bought in most major supermarkets but if you can't find them, substitute 3 or 4 large fresh chillies. If the sauce is too thick, let down to desired consistency with water.

PREPARATION TIME: 10 MINUTES + PLUS COOLING

COOKING TIME: 5 MINUTES

SERVES 6

100ml (4fl oz) rice vinegar
50g (2oz) sugar
1/2 jar peppadew peppers, drained
2 Tbsp light soy sauce

1 Put the vinegar and sugar in a small pan and heat gently until the sugar dissolves. Add the peppadew peppers and soy sauce simmer for 5 minutes. Remove from the heat and leave to cool.

2 Purée in a blender and store (for up to 1 week) in a covered container in the refrigerator until needed.

Piccalilli

The mustard sauce may separate a little when left to stand in the jars, so stir before serving if necessary. This pickle goes well with sausages, burgers and plain grilled meats.

PREPARATION TIME: 30 MINUTES + PLUS BRINING

COOKING TIME: ABOUT 15 MINUTES

MAKES APPROX. 2.7KG (6LB)

225g (8oz) green beans, cut into 2.5cm (1in) lengths
450g (1lb) shallots or button onions, peeled
1 green pepper, deseeded and cut into small chunks
1/4 cucumber, cut into small chunks
225g (8oz) courgettes, cut into small chunks
450g (1lb) cauliflower, divided into small florets
225g (8oz) salt
2.2L (4pt) cold water
115g (4oz) caster sugar
50g (2oz) cornflour
50g (2oz) mustard powder
1 Tbsp ground turmeric
1.1L (2pt) distilled malt vinegar

1 Place all the prepared vegetables in a large bowl. Add the salt to the cold water and pour over. Put a plate on top to make sure all the vegetables are submerged in the brine and leave to stand for 24 hours.

2 Drain the vegetables and rinse them very thoroughly to remove the brine by placing a few at a time in a sieve and running cold water over them.

3 Whisk the sugar, cornflour, mustard poweder and turmeric with a little of the vinegar until smooth. Pour into a large saucepan, stir in the remaining vinegar and bring to the boil, stirring occasionally.

4 Add the vegetables and simmer for about 10 minutes until they are starting to soften but are still a little crisp. Spoon into clean warm jars, packing the vegetables down well and spooning the sauce over them. Seal and store for at least 2 weeks before eating. Once opened store in the fridge, and eat within 2 weeks of opening.

Guacamole

To check if an avocado is ripe, hold the fruit in the palm of your hand and squeeze it gently by wrapping your fingers around it. The flesh should feel tender and give a little under the pressure. To speed the ripening of a hard avocado, store it in a warm place such as the airing cupboard.

PREPARATION TIME: 15 MINUTES

SERVES 4

2 medium-sized tomatoes, deseeded and finely chopped
1 shallot, peeled and grated or finely chopped
1–2 green chillies, deseeded and finely chopped
1 Tbsp lime or lemon juice
Salt
Paprika
2 ripe avocados

1 In a bowl, mix together the tomatoes, shallot and chillies with the lime or lemon juice. Season with salt and a little paprika. Cover and set aside for 1–2 hours to give the flavours time to develop.

2 About 30 minutes before serving, halve the avocados, remove the stones and, using a spoon, scoop out the flesh into a bowl. Coarsely mash the flesh with a fork and mix into the tomato and shallot mixture.

3 Spoon into a serving bowl and chill until required.

tip

If you need to have this ready more than about half an hour before serving, push the avocado stone into the finished dip and press clingfilm over the surface to help prevent it discolouring.

Romesco sauce

This is a tangy tomato sauce from Spain that makes an excellent accompaniment to grilled meats, fish, vegetables and burgers. The fried bread crumbs help thicken the sauce and add extra flavour.

PREPARATION TIME: 15 MINUTES

COOKING TIME: LESS THAN 10 MINUTES

SERVES 4

Approx. 150ml (5fl oz) olive oil
1 thick slice white bread
65g (2¹/₂ oz) ground almonds
2 garlic cloves, peeled and crushed
2 roasted red peppers, from a jar or deli counter
1 x 230g (8oz) tin plum tomatoes
1 tsp smoked paprika
2 Tbsp red wine vinegar

1 Heat 2 Tbsp olive oil in a frying pan and fry the bread until golden on both sides. Remove, add the ground almonds to the pan and cook for a couple of minutes or until they start to turn golden, turning them over frequently so they colour evenly. Remove and set aside.

2 Break up the bread into pieces and place in a food processor or blender with the almonds, garlic, peppers, tomatoes and their juice, paprika and wine vinegar. Process to a coarse purée, then add as much of the remaining oil, as necessary, until the sauce is the desired thick-mayonnaise-like consistency.

tip

If making the sauce in a food processor, drizzle tablespoonfuls of the oil down the feeder tube with the motor running, stopping the machine after each addition to check on the consistency of the sauce.

Blue cheese and chive dressing

A tangy way to brighten up a simple green salad is with this American-style blue cheese dressing. Serve it spooned over a mix of leaves including baby spinach, Cos lettuce and rocket or over chopped tomatoes, avocado and cucumber. It could also be served as an alternative dressing for the warm new potato, bacon and spring onion salad (see page 143).

PREPARATION TIME: 5 MINUTES

SERVES 4

175g (6oz) crumbly blue cheese, e.g. Roquefort or Stilton
3 Tbsp soured cream
2 Tbsp white wine vinegar
4 Tbsp olive oil
1 Tbsp snipped fresh chives
Freshly ground black pepper

1 Put all the ingredients in a food processor and whizz until smooth. If you don't have a food processor, mash the cheese in a bowl. Whisk the other ingredients together in another bowl and gradually beat in the cheese until evenly combined.

2 Cover the dressing with clingfilm and keep for up to 2 or 3 days in the refrigerator until needed.

tip

As the blue cheese has such a strong flavour, use a light olive oil rather than extra virgin, which would be too heavy. Sunflower oil or grapeseed oil would also be fine.

Cream cheese and sun-blushed tomato dip

Sun-blushed or semi-dried tomatoes are softer and sweeter than ones that have been fully dried, which can be quite hard and bitter. Usually packed in olive oil, sun-blushed tomatoes are available in jars or from deli counters.

PREPARATION TIME: 10 MINUTES

SERVES 4

150g (5oz) cream cheese
100ml (3¹/₂fl oz) soured cream
1 tsp Dijon mustard
8 sun-blushed tomatoes, finely chopped
2 Tbsp snipped fresh chives
1 Tbsp chopped fresh parsley

1 Mash the cream cheese until smooth and then beat in the soured cream and mustard until combined.

2 Stir in the sun-blushed tomatoes and half the herbs.

3 Spoon into a bowl, scatter over the remaining herbs and chill until ready to serve.

 tip

You can reduce the calories in this dip by using a low fat cream cheese and substituting Greek yogurt or half-fat crème fraiche for the soured cream.

Spicy peanut dipping sauce

The traditional accompaniment to satays, this sauce also goes well with plainly grilled pork chops and chicken breasts or stir-fried vegetables. If you make the sauce ahead and it thickens too much on standing, dilute down to the right consistency with warm water.

PREPARATION TIME: 5 MINUTES

COOKING TIME: LESS THAN 10 MINUTES

SERVES 8

2 Tbsp oil
3 shallots, peeled and very finely chopped
5 Tbsp crunchy peanut butter
2 Tbsp dark soy sauce
Juice of 2 limes
1–2 tsp fresh chilli purée
300ml (10fl oz) coconut milk

1 Heat the oil in a pan on a conventional hob and fry the shallots until softened but not browned.

2 Add the peanut butter, soy sauce, lime juice and chilli purée and stir until evenly mixed.

3 Gradually stir in the coconut milk until it is incorporated into the sauce.

3 Serve warm or at room temperature. It will keep in the fridge for up to 1 week, but will need reheating with a little water before serving.

tip

If you want a sauce with a chunkier texture, stir 50g (2oz) finely chopped roasted, unsalted peanuts in at the end. For a smoother sauce, use smooth peanut butter.

Tzatziki

Greek yogurt is creamier than other yogurts as excess water is strained out of it. If you use ordinary yogurt for this dip, make it as close to serving as you can so it doesn't become too "wet".

PREPARATION TIME: 15 MINUTES + PLUS DRAINING

SERVES 6

$^1/_2$ cucumber, peeled and coarsely grated
1 tsp salt
200g (7oz) natural Greek yogurt
2–3 garlic cloves, peeled and crushed
2 Tbsp chopped fresh mint

1 Put the grated cucumber in a sieve over a bowl, sprinkle with the salt and leave to drain for 30 minutes, pressing the cucumber with kitchen paper from time to time to remove as much water from it as possible.

2 Rinse the cucumber and pat dry with kitchen paper.

3 Put the yogurt in a bowl and stir in the garlic, cucumber and mint.

tip

You can use this same basic recipe to make raita, the yogurt-based dip from India served with tandoori dishes. Stir in 1 tablespoon chopped fresh coriander with the mint and dust the top with a little ground cardamom, chilli powder or crushed saffron threads. The cucumber can be finely diced rather than grated, if preferred.

Cucumber, carrot and white radish relish

This is an Oriental-style pickle that goes well with grilled meats such as the Herb and spice-rubbed steaks (see page 101) and Fragrant Asian lamb cutlets (see page 99).

PREPARATION TIME: 10 MINUTES + STANDING

SERVES 4

$^{1}/_{2}$ cucumber, coarsely grated
1 tsp salt
1 large carrot, coarsely grated
7.5cm (3in) piece white radish (daikon), peeled and
   coarsely grated
2 tsp sesame oil or few drops toasted sesame oil
2 tsp sesame seeds

1 Put the grated cucumber in a colander and set over a bowl to catch any water that drips out. Sprinkle with salt and leave to stand for 30 minutes.

2 Rinse the cucumber, pat dry with kitchen paper and mix with the grated carrot and white radish.

3 Drizzle over the sesame oil and sprinkle with the sesame seeds before serving.

tip

If you have an oriental food store nearby, buy black sesame seeds to sprinkle over the vegetables as they make an attractive garnish. If you only have the more common white sesame seeds, toast them lightly in a dry frying pan first to bring out their flavour and aroma.

Pepper, tomato and sweetcorn relish

This relish could be served with the Indonesian pork and chicken satay (see page 66) as an alternative to peanut sauce, and it also makes a good relish for burgers.

PREPARATION TIME: 10 MINUTES

COOKING TIME: 15 MINUTES

SERVES 6–8

1 red pepper, deseeded
1 Tbsp olive oil
4 spring onions, trimmed and finely chopped
1 garlic clove, peeled and crushed
1 tsp chilli sauce
175g (6oz) sweetcorn kernels, defrosted if frozen, drained if tinned
300ml (10fl oz) chunky tomato pasta sauce, from a jar or a tub from the
    chiller cabinet
1 tsp dried basil
Salt and pepper

1 Chop the red pepper into roughly the same size pieces as the sweetcorn kernels. Heat the oil in a pan on a conventional hob and fry the onions, pepper and garlic over a low heat until softened.

2 Mix in the chilli sauce, sweetcorn, pasta sauce, basil and seasoning and simmer for 10 minutes or until any excess liquid has evaporated, stirring occasionally. Serve warm or cold.

Avocado, pineapple and kidney bean salsa

Kidney beans need a good rinse under cold running water to get rid of the liquid that sticks to them during the canning process. You can ring the changes by making this dish with other beans such as borlotti, cannelloni or black eye peas, or a can of mixed beans.

PREPARATION TIME: 10 MINUTES

SERVES 6

1 x 400g (14oz) tin red kidney beans
12 cherry tomatoes, halved
2 pineapple rings, chopped
1 avocado, peeled and chopped
1 green chilli, deseeded and finely chopped
2 Tbsp white wine vinegar

1 Drain the kidney beans into a sieve and rinse thoroughly by running cold water over them.

2 Mix the beans with the other ingredients and spoon into a bowl.

 ## tip

If you're making the salsa several hours ahead, leave out the avocado and add it just before serving to prevent it turning brown.

Mango, red onion and cucumber salsa

Salsas are designed to cool down hot, spicy dishes but as they usually include chilli, their cooling effect is not as effective as it might be! They do, however, provide a fresh, crunchy contrast to grilled meat and fish. Jalapeños are large, pale green chillies from Mexico. They have a fairly mild flavour and can be bought pickled in tins or jars from most major supermarkets.

PREPARATION TIME: 10 MINUTES

SERVES 4

1 mango, peeled and flesh finely diced
1 red onion, peeled and finely chopped
2 medium tomatoes, deseeded and finely diced
1/4 cucumber, deseeded and finely diced
1 green jalapeño chilli, deseeded and finely chopped
1 tsp sugar
3 Tbsp red wine vinegar

1 Mix the mango, red onion, tomatoes, cucumber and chilli together in a bowl. Stir the sugar into the vinegar until it dissolves and pour over the chopped ingredients.

2 Chill until ready to serve.

Spicy tomato sauce

A homemade 'ketchup' that can be used to dress up all sorts of things from plain grilled burgers, steaks, prawns and chicken, to the Tofu, red pepper, mushroom and courgette satay on page 121 or Pork balls on skewers (see page 55). Make the sauce the day before so the flavours have plenty of time to develop and become mellow.

PREPARATION TIME: 20 MINUTES

COOKING TIME: 40 MINUTES

SERVES 4–6

2 Tbsp sunflower oil
1 red onion, peeled and finely chopped
1 large carrot, grated
1 celery stick, sliced
1 large garlic clove, peeled and sliced
1 large red chilli, deseeded and finely chopped
1 x 400g (14oz) tin plum tomatoes
2 Tbsp lime juice
2 Tbsp light soy sauce
2 Tbsp tomato purée
4 Tbsp red wine
1 Tbsp light brown sugar

1 Heat the oil in a pan on a conventional hob, add the onion, carrot and celery and fry over a low heat until softened. Add the garlic and chilli and fry for 2 -3 minutes.

2 Stir in the tomatoes and their juice, the lime juice, soy, tomato purée, red wine and brown sugar, cover the pan and simmer gently for 30 minutes.

3 Liquidize in a blender or food processor until smooth.

 ## tip

If you have a glut of home grown tomatoes, these could be used instead of tinned but they must be ripe and full of flavour or the sauce will be bland. Remove the skins and pips first as if they are blitzed in a processor with the other ingredients, they'll give the sauce a sharp, bitter taste.

9 desserts

Banana splits
Sticky fruit kebabs
Bananas baked in their jackets with lemon
   cream
Baked apples with dates, oranges and
   pecans
Sticky coconut rice with lime and papaya
Toasted brioche with sunshine fruits
Melon and grape salad in ginger syrup
Brown sugar fruits
Orange and honey-baked figs
Passion fruit parcels

Banana splits

If you're cooking for the family, use orange juice and chocolate buttons to flavour the children's bananas instead of rum and cinnamon – just don't forget which ones are which!

PREPARATION TIME: 10 MINUTES

COOKING TIME: 6–8 MINUTES

SERVES 6

6 large ripe but firm bananas
50g (2oz) butter, cut into small dice
3 Tbsp soft brown sugar
Juice of 1 lemon
6 Tbsp white rum
1 tsp ground cinnamon

1 Using a sharp knife, cut the unpeeled bananas in half lengthways. Cut six sheets of foil, each large enough to enclose a banana comfortably, and place two halves on each.

2 Spoon the butter, brown sugar, lemon juice, rum and cinnamon on top of the two halves of each banana, re-shape roughly and wrap the foil around, sealing the edges of each parcel tightly.

3 Cook the parcels on the grill rack for 6–8 minutes or until the bananas are soft but still holding their shape. Open the parcels carefully and eat the bananas straight from the foil, scooping out the flesh with a spoon and basting the juices over each mouthful.

To prepare the bananas for children: make in the same way, but put chocolate buttons between the banana halves instead of butter, sugar and cinnamon and spoon orange juice over them, instead of rum.

tip

You could use dark rum instead of white but cut down on the quantity of sugar or leave it out altogether as dark is much sweeter. Other Caribbean spirits or liqueurs such as Curaçao, Tia Maria or Malibu could also be used.

Sticky fruit kebabs

Use any selection of fruit you like for these colourful skewers. Although the fruit needs to be ripe, it should be firm as well so it doesn't collapse as soon as it goes on the chiminea rack. Serve warm with thick cream or ice cream.

PREPARATION TIME: 10 MINUTES

COOKING TIME: 5 MINUTES

SERVES 4

8 large strawberries
1 banana, peeled and cut into chunks
2 peaches, stoned and each cut into 8 wedges
4 apricots, stoned and halved
2 kiwi fruit, peeled and each cut into 4 chunks
4 Tbsp maple syrup
50g (2oz) butter, melted
$1/2$ tsp ground cinnamon
$1/2$ tsp ground allspice

TO SERVE
Thick cream or ice cream

1 Spear the strawberries, banana, peaches, apricots and kiwi fruit alternately on to four long or eight short skewers.

2 Mix together the maple syrup, melted butter and spices and brush over the fruit.

3 Cook on the grill rack for 5 minutes, turning the skewers over several times, until the fruit is lightly scorched.

 ## tip

Instead of maple syrup, you could use clear honey or golden syrup, mixed with a little lemon juice to take the edge off its sweetness. Warm the honey or golden syrup with the other ingredients first so it becomes more liquid and easier to brush over the fruit.

Bananas baked in their jackets with lemon cream

The easiest barbecue dessert by far. The bananas are simply placed on the chiminea grill and roasted until their skins turn a rich mahogany brown and their flesh is soft and sweet. Limoncello is a fragrant – and strong! – lemon liqueur from Sorrento near Naples, a region of Italy famous for its orchards of lemon trees which produce large, juicy fruit.

PREPARATION TIME: 5 MINUTES

COOKING TIME: 10 MINUTES

SERVES 8

150ml (5fl oz) double cream
Finely grated rind of 1 lemon
2 Tbsp limoncello liqueur (optional)
8 large ripe but firm bananas

1 Whip the cream until it just holds its shape. Add the lemon rind and limoncello, if using, and whip until the cream is thick. Chill for at least 1 hour so the flavours can develop.

2 Put the bananas on the grill rack and cook for about 10 minutes, turning them over regularly, until the skins turn dark brown and are starting to split.

3 Leave diners to peel their own bananas and let them spoon the lemon cream over the soft, fragrant fruit inside.

Baked apples with dates, oranges and pecans

These can be prepared in advance ready to be popped on the chiminea rack and left to cook once the main course has been served.

PREPARATION TIME: 15 MINUTES

COOKING TIME: 20–25 MINUTES

SERVES 4

4 large cooking apples, e.g. Bramley
2 seedless oranges, segmented and chopped
8 dates, stoned and chopped
50g (2oz) chopped pecans
2 Tbsp clear honey
50g (2oz) butter, melted
150ml (5fl oz) orange or apple juice

1 Using an apple corer, remove the cores and seeds from the apples. With a sharp knife slit the skin around the centre of each.

2 Place each apple on a sheet of greased foil large enough to enclose it comfortably. Mix together the orange segments, dates, pecans, honey and melted butter and spoon into the centre of the apples, packing the mixture down tightly.

3 Gather the foil around the apples and spoon over the orange or apple juice. Fold over the edges of the foil to make neat parcels and cook the apples on the grill rack for 20–25 minutes or until they are tender. Serve warm.

tip

Make sure the apples are tightly wrapped in greased foil so they don't stick to it and none of the delicious juices leak out. Alternatively, stand the apples side by side in a roasting tin or other fireproof dish and overwrap it with foil, sealing the edges tightly.

Sticky coconut rice with lime and papaya

Also known as "glutinous rice", Thai sticky rice has short white grains that, as the name suggests, stick together once they are cooked. It can be bought in supermarkets that stock Thai ingredients or Asian food shops. The recipe needs to be started the day before as the rice should be left to soak for 4–5 hours or overnight.

PREPARATION TIME: 15 MINUTES + SOAKING AND STANDING

COOKING TIME: 20–25 MINUTES

SERVES 4

200g (7oz) sticky rice
175ml (6fl oz) coconut milk
1 papaya, peeled, deseeded and sliced
8 lychees, peeled and stoned
Finely grated rind and rind of 2 limes

1 Put the rice in a bowl and pour over enough cold water to cover it by 5cm (2in). Leave to soak for several hours or overnight.

2 Drain the rice thoroughly. Line a steamer with muslin or a clean J-cloth and spread the rice out in it. Steam on top of the chiminea for 20–25 minutes or until the rice is tender and sticky.

3 Scrape the rice out of the steamer into a bowl, warm the coconut milk and mix into the rice. Leave to stand for 15 minutes.

4 Serve with the papaya and lychees with the rind sprinkled over the rice and the lime juice over the fruit.

 ## tip

Soaking the rice for several hours cuts down on the time it needs to steam and become tender. The water in the steamer needs to be kept at a constant simmer, so top it up with boiling water or increase the cooking time if necessary.

Toasted brioche with sunshine fruits

Instead of brioche, slices of any sweet fruit loaf could be used, or even halved and toasted hot-cross buns.

PREPARATION TIME: 10 MINUTES

COOKING TIME: 10 MINUTES

SERVES 4

8 fresh or tinned peach halves
50g (2oz) butter
50g (2oz) soft brown sugar
1 Tbsp lemon juice
1 mango, peeled and sliced
175g (6oz) strawberries, hulled and halved or quartered if large
4 slices brioche, lightly toasted
2 Tbsp toasted almonds

1 Cut the peach halves in half to make 16 thick slices. Melt the butter in a large frying pan on top of the chiminea, add the sugar and lemon juice and stir until the sugar dissolves.

2 Let the mixture bubble for 1 minute, then add the peaches, mango slices and strawberries, spooning the pan juices over the fruit until it is well coated. Leave to simmer whilst you prepare the brioche.

3 Cut each slice of brioche into two triangles and place on serving plates. Spoon over the fruit and caramelized juices and sprinkle with the flaked almonds.

4 Serve immediately with pouring cream or ice cream.

 ## tip

If using fresh peaches, skin them first by placing in a bowl and pouring over boiling water to cover. Leave to stand for a couple of minutes, drain then slit the skins with a sharp knife and strip off the skins.

Melon and grape salad in ginger syrup

You can use other types of melon, but this dessert looks most attractive when you mix as many varieties as you can that have different coloured flesh. If you're not keen on ginger, flavour the syrup with a cinnamon stick or ½ tsp ground cinnamon.

PREPARATION TIME: 15 MINUTES

COOKING TIME: LESS THAN 5 MINUTES

SERVES 8

1 cantaloupe melon
1 ogen melon
1 large wedge of watermelon
200g (7oz) mixed red and green seedless grapes
2 Tbsp soft brown sugar
4 Tbsp lemon juice
2 pieces crystallized stem ginger, cut into very fine shreds

1 Halve, deseed and peel the cantaloupe and ogen melons. Cut the flesh into bite-sized pieces. Remove any seeds from the watermelon, peel and cut into bite-sized pieces. Place in a heatproof serving dish and add the grapes.

2 Pour 350ml (12fl oz) water into a pan and add the sugar. Heat on the top of the chiminea, stirring frequently until the sugar dissolves. Simmer for a couple of minutes and then stir in the lemon juice and stem ginger.

3 Leave the syrup to cool a little before pouring over the melon and grapes.

 ## tip

To test if a melon is ripe, press the opposite end to the stalk with your thumbs and the flesh should give a little. The melon should also have a sweet, fragrant scent.

Brown sugar fruits

These fruits are delicious served with crème fraîche, double cream or vanilla ice cream.

PREPARATION TIME: 15 MINUTES

COOKING TIME: 5 MINUTES

SERVES 4

75g (3oz) unsalted butter
75g (3oz) dark muscovado or dark soft brown sugar
4 Tbsp dark rum
Finely grated rind and juice of 1 small orange
Finely grated rind and juice of 1 lemon
2 pineapple rings, cut into chunks
1 mango, peeled and sliced
175g (6oz) lychees, peeled and stoned
1 banana, peeled and sliced

TO SERVE
Crème fraîche, double cream or vanilla ice cream

1 Heat a frying pan on top of the chiminea, add the butter and, when melted, stir in the brown sugar, rum, orange rind and juice and lemon rind and juice.

2 When the sugar has dissolved, let the syrup bubble for 3–4 minutes.

3 Add the fruit and simmer for a further 1–2 minutes, basting the fruit with the pan juices. Serve the fruit straight from the pan with the juices spooned over.

tip

Make sure the sugar dissolves before the sauce comes to the boil or you'll end up with an unpleasantly gritty syrup. Don't let the fruit bubble for too long in the syrup or the banana pieces could become too soft and disintegrate. Other fruits could be added to the mix such as pears, apples or strawberries.

Orange and honey-baked figs

Vanilla extract is the strongest of the liquid vanilla flavourings, the finest coming from the island of Madagascar in the Indian Ocean. If you use the less strong vanilla essence, increase the quantity to ½ tsp. The figs need to be ripe but still firm and cutting a cross in the top of each fruit helps them absorb the sticky citrus juices.

PREPARATION TIME: 10 MINUTES

COOKING TIME: 15 MINUTES

SERVES 4

8 fresh figs
4 Tbsp clear honey
Few drops vanilla extract
100ml (3¹/₂fl oz) fresh orange juice
2 Tbsp finely chopped pistachios
Finely grated rind of 1 orange

TO SERVE
Thick Greek yoghurt, crème fraîche or ice cream

1 Cut a cross in the top of each fig with a sharp knife and stand the figs in a single layer in a shallow baking tray, just large enough to take all the figs.

2 Stir the honey, vanilla extract and orange juice together and pour over the figs. Bake, uncovered, on the grill rack for 15 minutes or until the figs are tender, basting them once or twice with the juices in the tray.

3 Serve warm, with the chopped pistachios and finely grated orange rind sprinkled over, and accompanied by Greek yoghurt, crème fraîche or ice cream.

Passion fruit parcels

Serve these parcels straight from the grill rack, leaving diners to open their own and spoon in liberal amounts of cream or ice cream as they prefer.

PREPARATION TIME: 15 MINUTES

COOKING TIME: 10 MINUTES

SERVES 4

1 papaya, peeled, deseeded and chopped
1 star fruit, sliced
1 peach, stoned and sliced
2 pineapple rings, chopped
1 banana, peeled and sliced
8 strawberries, hulled and halved if large
2 passion fruit
4 Tbsp soft brown sugar
8 Tbsp white wine
1 tsp ground cinnamon
50g (2oz) butter, cut into small pieces

TO SERVE
Cream or ice cream

1 Divide the prepared papaya, star fruit, peach, pineapple, banana and strawberries between four sheets of foil. Halve the passion fruit and scoop out the seeds and pulp on top, dividing it between the four servings.

2 Spoon 1 Tbsp brown sugar and 2 Tbsp white wine over each serving and sprinkle with a little cinnamon. Dot with the butter and seal each parcel tightly by gathering the foil around the fruit and folding over the edges.

3 Place on the grill rack for about 10 minutes to heat through. Open up and serve with cream or ice cream.